European Cannabis Cultivation

Published in the UK by

Avalon Wholesale Ltd.
Southsea, Hants

In The USA by

Green Candy Press
San Francisco, CA

ISBN 09541855-2-8

Editor: Jay Walker
Typography: H. Bennett
Graphics and Layout: Bad Company Design UK
Pictures: ©Mel Thomas, Nol van Schaik, Pepper Design USA, Shantibaba, Hugh Wilson, London Cabbie (S), Gypsy Nirvana, Barge photography, Ajust-A-Wings Australia and Bud Good

Dedicated to the thousands of men and women serving prison sentences for cannabis

Case Outline

On 29 November police searched the premises. They discovered that a large area within the premises had been concealed behind a secret door and contained a sophisticated hydroponic growing environment with dehumidifiers, lighting and irrigation facilities professionally wired in and bypassing the metered supply. The growing area was 600 square metres enabling 6 crops per annum of 300KG of cannabis to be produced. 'Skunk' cannabis is priced at £6 per gram - £1.8 million potential per annum or at a low wholesale cost of £2,000 per kilo - £600,000. Based on the amount of equipment found at the premises it is estimated that electricity valued at £26,520 had been used. Aggravating features are very high value of cannabis produced from the 2 factories, highly professional operation for large scale production of controlled drug.

Record of Tape Recorded Interview

411. "Right, Mr. Big takes you there, what electrics did you actually complete within the building?"
R. "I, er done ring main circuits, which is sockets"
411. "I actually asked you the question earlier, who were you working for?"
R. "I will refer to that person as Mr. Big"
411. "Do you not wish to give me his real name?"
R. "I'm concerned about my family's and, er my personal safety"
411. "Who purchased the equipment?"
R. "Mr. Big from [redacted]s Electrical Suppliers"
411. "So you are confirming Mr. Big collected the equipment?"
R. "Yes, Yes"

HMP [redacted]

APPLICATION FOR VISITOR TO BE INCLUDED ON LIST OF APPROVED VISITORS TO A CATEGORY A INMATE

NAME OF PRISONER
(NAME TO BE ENTERED BY PRISON)..

The above who is a prisoner in this prison, has asked that you be allowed to visit him. If you wish to visit him you will have to be placed on his approved visitors list. For this purpose you will please complete the enclosed form and return it, enclosing 2 passport size photographs. The photographs must be full face without a hat. After I have received the forms you will receive a visit from the police who will seek verification that you are the person named as the visitor. The Home Office will make the final decision as to your approval. If you are refused no reason may be given. If and when you are approved, the above named prisoner will be informed and he can then send you a visiting order.

Yours Faithfully

Security Department
(For the Governor, HMP [redacted]l)
Encs: Approved Visitor Application Form.

CONTENTS

DRUGS RING SMASHED

FOUR men were expected to appear before [redacted] magistrates today in connection with a multi-million pound drug factory found when armed police raided a disused warehouse.

The men were arrested and brought to [redacted] following raids on properties in Luton, Watford, Bristol, Hackney, Harrow and [redacted] in [redacted] where another drug factory was discovered.

Three other men and three women were also arrested during Operation Vortex which involved 31 officers from [redacted] along with police from Bedfords Hertfordshire, Bristol, Aylebury, Metropolitan police and the South Regional Crime Squad.

The four faced questioning in relati large scale cannabis factory found in [redacted], [redacted], [redacted] November last year.

Detective Inspector [redacted] of [redacted] police said, "the searc and arrest phase of Operation Vortex wei very well with all the suspects arrested an the seizure of a large volume of exhibits and documents along with varying amounts of drugs, notably the live factory of more than 600 plants in [redacted]"

But [redacted] said " the factory discovered in [redacted] last year had a far larger capacity than the one found yesterday. Hydroponics factories can produce £1 million street value of drugs per year and make huge profits for criminals who run them.

However they also demand much equipment, electricity and power, which is usually obtained dishonestly"

FACTORY-Police uncovered a cannabis manufacturing plant

Detective I

paid £45.000 in cash for the warehouse in a quiet side street. The gang installed sophisticated growing equipment, including dehumidifiers, powerful lighting and irrigation systems.

'Tardis'

The 475 square meters warehouse was code-named 'Tardis' by the gang because the small frontage concealed a much larger interior. They also by-passed the electricity meter to avoid an estimated bill of £26.000.

'factory for cannabis'

FOREWORD

I've been in jail and I am a little bored. Tom Horne. 1904

The Author of this book was a notorious European cannabis cultivator based in London. Code-named Mr. Big by detectives he was eventually arrested after a covert operation involving four separate police forces and charged with conspiring to produce 2.5 million pounds worth of skunk cannabis. The trial judge called him "A horticultural expert involved in a resolute and successful attempt to produce cannabis on a commercial scale". The Author and his co-accused were sentenced to more than 14 years imprisonment between them and ordered to pay over £150,000 in fines or serve an additional three years without parole. Convicted of producing cannabis he was held as a category 'A' prisoner on a maximum-security wing in one of Europe's most secure jails. This book was conceived in that prison.

The author now lives quietly in Amsterdam.

Also by the author:
Cannabis Cultivation (North American version)

Preflowers

Preflowers are initially tiny and impossible to distinguish without a magnifying glass or 10x loupe. They generally appear above the 4th node, after the 4th week of seed growth, the female preflower is pear shaped and produces 2 pistils / some female preflowers never produce pistils. A female preflower without pistils is difficult to distinguish from a male

Female flowers

Female flowers are distinguished from their male counterparts by tiny, white, hair like pistils that appear (usually in pairs) from bulbous pods at each branch union. Male plants do not produce any pistils. Crops grown from seed will consist of 50% female and 50% male plants so growers take female cuttings to ensure an all female/sinsemilla crop

Male flowers

Male plants will show earlier than the females. Male flowers form in clusters of small, green balls on stalks that open to reveal tiny white petals. The flowers release pollen to fertilize the females before the plant itself dies back. Male plants can be identified by the preflowers well before they shed pollen. Male plants must be immediately removed from the crop

Chapter 1

CANNABIS SATIVA

I know the grass beyond the door, the sweet keen smell. Dante Rossetti. 1828–1882

Cannabis along with hemp is a member of the *Moraceae* family. There are three distinct varieties of cannabis that are grown for their Tetrahydrocannabinol or THC content: *Cannabis sativa*, *Cannabis indica* and *Cannabis ruderalis*.

Cannabis sativa

These plants are characterized by long thin flowers and spiky leaves. They originate from equatorial regions where the growing season is hotter. They are not generally used for outdoor cultivation in colder, damper climates, although some hybrids can produce reasonable yields in these conditions. *Cannabis sativas* have more of a high than *Cannabis indica* buds.

Cannabis indica

These plants originated in the Hindu Kush areas of Central Asia, where the weather is changeable and growing conditions can be harsh. Hardy plants, they mature early and are characterized by broad, short leaves and heavy, tight flowers. *C.Indica* varieties are ideal for indoor and outdoor cultivation in Europe.

Cannabis ruderalis

Ruderalis is a variety of cannabis that grows wild in parts of Eastern Europe and Russia. It is characterised by its early flowering, with some plants starting irrespective of the photoperiod. *Ruderalis* is ideal for cultivation in cooler climates with changeable conditions. There are hybrid varieties available that combine *C. ruderalis* and *C. indica.*

Cannabis is **dioecious,** which means the plant is either male (staminate) or female (pistillate), although genetically unstable **hermaphrodites** with both male and female flowers do occur. Sexual reproduction is carried out by the female flower in the ovaries at the base of the pistils, containing the female germ cells. Fertilization occurs when male pollen unites with female ovules.

Cannabis regulates its development and flower production by measuring the length of daylight falling onto its leaves. It produces a light-sensitive hormone called phytochrome that is responsible for altering the plant from vegetative growth into flowering when it reaches a critical level. Cannabis plants change from the vegetative state into the flowering cycle when they receive 12 hours of uninterrupted darkness. They will respond to this change no matter where they are grown, even under artificial lighting. Cultivators can use this response to their advantage by controlling the plants' day length, either by changing the lighting cycles or by covering outdoor and greenhouse plants. Plants that are grown under lighting are given 18 to 24 hours of daylight to keep them in the vegetative stage. Plants given 24 hours of daylight will grow 25% faster. There is no requirement for them to sleep; however, the grower needs to calculate the cost in terms of electricity used. If there is a problem with consuming excessive amounts then the cycle should be run at 18 hours for best results. Cuttings under fluorescents respond better to 24 hours of daylight.

Only the female flower produces buds, and there is no difference in the potency of plants that are flowered at different ages, younger plants just yield less. Once the flowering cycle has been induced a young plant will have the same THC content as an older one. THC is the name given to the cannabinoids, found in cannabis plants, which are unique to the species. They are not found anywhere else and although we can synthesize them in the laboratory, they are a poor imitation of natural THC. These cannabinoids are actually made up of several different but related chemicals with similar effects. They are known as CBN, THCV, CBV and CBDV. There is also one chemical – labelled CBD – that is known to block the psycho-active effect of the others. Some plants will have all sets of chemicals in their make-up, and there are several different versions of THC found in differing plants, so in practice we label these all as THC.

The THC drug is principally contained in multicellular structures on the surface of the flower heads and smaller leaves called *stalked capitate trichome glands*. These appear as tiny, translucent, mushroom-like structures that are visible through a magnifying glass. The heads of these structures contain oil that is secreted as a sticky resin and that contains high levels of THC.

The glands are not the only multicellular structures on the plant's surface. Bulbous glands, also known as sessile glands, are found on some of the leaves and contain low levels of cannabinoids. The other structures to look out for are unicellular hairs that actually look like short hairs, and cystolith hairs, which appear pointed under the magnifying glass and contain calcium carbonate deposits. Neither of these two structures contains any cannabinoids.

The male develops small clusters of white flowers that release pollen before dropping from the plant. The male dies shortly after the flowers drop. Male plants have low quantities of THC and are usually removed from the crop to prevent the pollination of the females. Once a female has been pollinated all her efforts go into seed production, which is not what cannabis producers want. By leaving the female unpollinated you get thicker, more resinous buds whose weight is composed of flower material, not seeds. The Spanish word for seedless cannabis is "Sinsemilla," and this is what gives these harvests their name.

In order to ensure an all-female crop, most cultivators take cuttings from a known female and grow genetically identical clones as opposed to seedlings. If you have a crop of seedlings you can identify the females once flowering has started by their small white hair-like pistils emerging from bulbous pods at every branch union. The males produce small green balls that will develop into flowers.

The structure of the cannabis plant stem is of interest to cultivators. Directly underneath the green bark are two layers responsible for the transportation of water and nutrients between the leaves and the plant. The leaves are basically sugar factories where sunlight is collected and used in the production of energy. Sugars and *phosphitides* are produced by combining this energy with carbon dioxide from the atmosphere and nutrients from the soil. The layer directly beneath the outer bark is called the ***phloem*** and its tissues are used by the plant to conduct food processed in the leaves back down into the plant itself. Beneath this there is another layer called the ***xylem,*** which is responsible for conducting water and nutrients back up to the leaves to be used in the production of sugars.

We can use the structure of the plant stem to our advantage when carrying out ***asexual propagation***. It is possible to reduce the stress to the mother plant and cuttings by using a technique known as ***air layering***. This method involves creating a clone, complete with roots that is still attached to the parent plant. We do this with a little careful surgery on the clone site. By cutting into the phloem and disrupting the flow of nutrients away from the selected area, while leaving the xylem intact and still feeding the newly developing clone. When the drain of food back into the mother is shut off the clone is able to utilize it in the production of new roots. The clone will be a complete genetic copy of the mother, inheriting all of the same characteristics.

Cannabis inherits its characteristics from its parent plants. When sexual reproduction takes place, male and female germ cells join together. Every plant cell contains chromosomes that hold genetic information. Each pair of chromosomes contains two genes for each characteristic: cannabis plants have 10 pairs of chromosomes, making a total of 20. Plants that contain these normal sets of chromosomes are called *Diploid.* Abnormal numbers of chromosomes within one plant cell are generally referred to as *Polyploid* plants.

Chapter 2

LOCATION

It comes down to three things; location, location, and location. Donald Trump

Artificial environments known as ***grow rooms*** offer the cannabis grower a safer alternative to outdoor cultivation, with the benefit of year-round consistent crops. Grow rooms can be built in a variety of locations and can vary in size from small cupboard or closet setups, to warehouse-sized cannabis farms. Your location needs to be secure and free of extremes of temperature or dampness, and requires a supply of water and electricity. Successful grow rooms can be built in both commercial and residential premises.

Residential

Spare rooms (bedrooms are ideal)
Attics and lofts (although these can suffer from excessive heat during the summer months)
Cellars (damp can become a problem in some cellars and basements)
Cupboards and closets
Outhouses and sheds (including greenhouses)
Garages
Mobile homes (including trailers and campers with access to power)
Apartments

Commercial

Industrial units
Warehouses
Office blocks (provided they are secure)
Agricultural buildings (such as barns and poultry units)
Lockup garages (power can sometimes be a problem in these setups)
Retail units (unused areas including living accommodation)

Horticultural units
Containers

The location and size of the grow room is determined by the crop that you want to produce. Cultivators interested in growing enough for their own consumption need only a small amount of space in which to grow their plants; a cupboard setup using low-wattage lighting can provide all they need. Those wanting to cultivate on a commercial scale will require premises where they can farm with rows of 1000-watt high-pressure sodium lights and automated hydroponics.
Having decided on the location, you can set about building an artificial environment in which to grow. All setups, regardless of size, have the same basic requirements.

Light *of the correct spectrum*
Water *at the correct temperature*
Nutrients *in the correct balance*
Air *rich in carbon dioxide and well-circulated*
Humidity and temperature *within the correct range*

To achieve this artificial environment you will supply light to the plants using artificial lighting, control the air, humidity and temperature with heaters, dehumidifiers, fans and carbon dioxide emitters, and deliver nutrients to the plants using fertilizers.

Preparing the Grow Room

Before installing the artificial environment, the grow room needs to be prepared. It is important to seal all windows and doors to prevent light contamination from outside. In residential locations, windows should be prepared by first hanging a net curtain or Venetian blind. Thin plywood is then sprayed with matt black paint and secured over the whole of the window opening, from the inside. Finally, tape along the edges with masking tape to ensure that the window is lightproof. When windows are viewed from the outside they appear black, so the board creates an optical illusion behind the net or blinds that is difficult to detect, even close up. The room appears as if it is empty and unlit.

If you are not using carbon dioxide emitters, and providing that it is not a downstairs or neighbour-facing window where odours may be detected, vents can be built into the plywood screen. However, you must ensure that you leave the window slightly open. Bend ducting twice through 90° to prevent light from escaping. If it's not possible to fix a vent into the window opening, use two lengths of ducting run from the best point of entry to give you an inlet and outlet vent, positioned at opposite ends of the room. The vents can be bathroom extractor fans, although these may be a little noisy for some setups. Silent-running extractors can be purchased and are definitely worth the additional cost. On longer duct runs you can install an inline fan to boost the flow.

Clean the grow room thoroughly, wiping down all surfaces with a diluted disinfectant or 5% bleach solution, then paint the walls white. Light distribution in a grow room is greatly increased by making all surfaces and walls reflective. White paint is up to 75% efficient at reflecting light from its surface. Mylar sheeting, available at most hydroponic suppliers, is a massive 95% efficient at reflecting light and can be used to cover the wall surfaces, or hung on a framework to make an enclosed, reflective tent. Alternatives to paint or Mylar sheeting are white plastic sheeting or aluminium foil. Use aluminium foil with the shiny side facing the wall to avoid hot spots. Mirrors should not be used as reflectors because they soak up light instead of bouncing it back onto the growing plants.

During daylight, shut the door to the grow room and stand in the darkened room – this way you will see any light that is not blocked out effectively and you can remedy the situation. Remember that light coming into the grow area will ruin your flowering cycle, and light shining out from the grow room can compromise your security. Areas to watch out for are leaks around windows and doors and cracks in the floors or brickwork. Use aluminium; or duct tape to seal leaks.

Light Sealing Windows

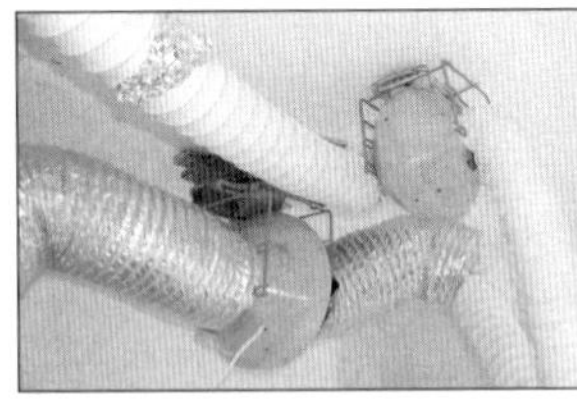

Inline fans vent the room

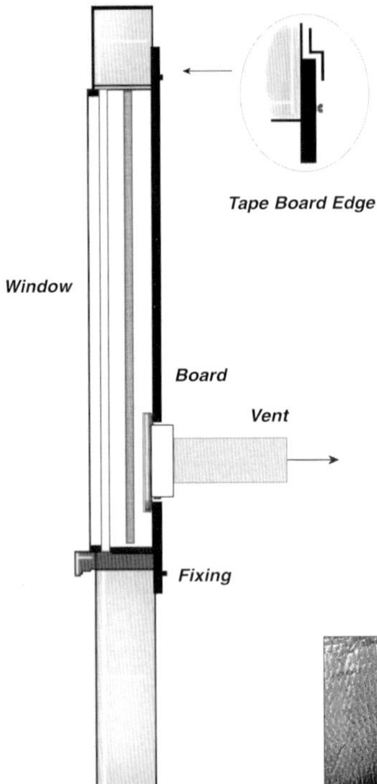

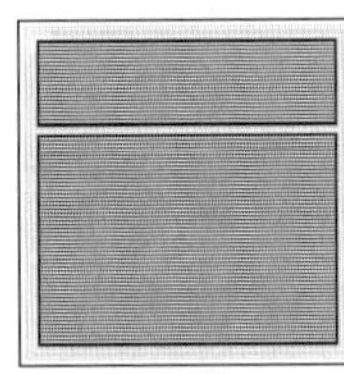

Front View

This ducting vents through the window board

Chapter 3

SECURITY

Three can keep a secret, if two of them are dead. Benjamin Franklin, 1706-1790

Whatever your requirements, the location of your grow room must be secret. If you're cultivating on a small scale at home, you must keep knowledge of your grow room confined to a need to know basis. If you have a larger setup away from home, you should take steps to avoid being followed.

Learning a few basic counter surveillance techniques can help keep you one step ahead of the authorities. If you live in a city or large town, keep authorities off your track as you move to and from your grow room by using public transportation (boarding buses and trains at the last possible moment) and by entering busy department stores and leaving by fire exits. Try to find routes that involve crossing pedestrian bridges or using underground pedestrian tunnels where anyone following you is channelled and forced into showing themselves. Constantly change your route.

If you have to drive to your grow room, take a route that involves moving through traffic lights and one way streets. Try to time your crossings as the lights change and make obvious diversions that a tailing vehicle can't copy without being noticed. Surveillance teams will use four or more vehicles to follow you, including motorcycles, so always try to be what the police term "surveillance aware." Find an area away from your home location where you can pull over and physically check the underbody of your vehicle, as modern tracking devices can be placed underneath and held in position by a series of small magnets. These devices have a range of over 9 km and are regularly used on police operations, along with satellite tracking systems that have unlimited range. Some tracking devices emit a signal that allows them to be located with hand-held devices that can be purchased from specialist suppliers. Or, have your vehicle swept by a reputable company to detect and eliminate eavesdropping and surveillance devices.

If you use a mobile (cell) phone, leave it at home whenever you visit your grow room. Even when switched off, cell phones emit a pulse signal, powered by their own internal battery, which is intended to link the phone to the nearest transmitter. The pulse signal can also provide the phone company with details of your movements that the police can and do use, both in surveillance operations and in court cases. Radio pagers can also be tracked but the company will have to contact your device in order to locate it. Therefore, if you are continually receiving test transmissions, it could indicate that you are under observation. The police regularly clone pagers to monitor a suspect's messages.

You should also avoid contacting associates (even people who are not involved in cannabis production) on your home phone or landline. Telephone tapping is used by police both legally, with the relevant court orders, and illegally. Most telephone surveillance is never mentioned in court cases and is used purely to collate information on you, so never discuss anything on your telephone. Part of police procedure is to link surveillance targets by the numbers that they telephone. The dates and times are noted and listed, which then helps the police intelligence teams to build a picture of your associates. They will produce this information in any subsequent court cases to link defendants. Use public pay phones when you need to contact someone, but be aware that surveillance teams are trained to wait near the pay phone, even queuing up while you are using it, so that they can be next to use the phone and to verify your call. They dial a specially established number that is constantly being changed, and an operator tells them all the connections that have been made from that phone. Although the police get the numbers, they can't record the conversation: by doubling back on yourself and watching for people who use the pay phone or phone booth after you, can frustrate their efforts. A friend of mine showed me statements a surveillance team had made about him. One officer wrote, "I waited outside of the phone booth, Smith finished his call and then left the booth, he held the door open for me and said, ' There's still credit left mate.' I waited, then verified all the calls he had made from that booth." Unaware he was under surveillance; my friend left phone credit for the officer, who used it to check the numbers he had called.

Voice activated recording equipment is used throughout Europe. By recording and analysing your speech patterns, then loading this information into the computer program, your calls can be intercepted by the telephone company. This is already in use in Amsterdam, Dublin and London. Keyword activation is also in use and flags specific words that you may use over the phone, such as 'cannabis'. Be aware that listening devices are routinely placed into suspected cannabis dealer's houses, often illegally, and the information gathered is collated and acted upon.

Avoid leaving fingerprints in your garden or on any equipment. This is not as relevant for small home producers, but anyone working on a larger scale should always wear gloves. The first thing police scenes of crime officers do when a cannabis factory has been discovered is to fingerprint every surface. Beware of bringing equipment into the grow room that you have handled away from the area, and do not touch any plastic bags you use to package and distribute dried buds: that's how growers are identified.

Remove all identification that can link your lights and equipment to any horticultural suppliers or the police will take statements from them. Not all will cooperate, but on my last conviction, statements from a UK hydroponics and cannabis seed supplier gave police details of every purchase I had made going back 18 months. Then the managing director allowed drug squad detectives to search the company's computer database to see if any of the defendants' names appeared on their mailing list. UK police officers even travelled to

Holland to speak to a major horticultural lighting manufacturer based there, as they had found several of their lights in our possession.

Police investigation teams will search for any paperwork that can be linked to you. Never keep written records of telephone numbers, addresses or even your crop's progress. Any financial dealings you have written down will be called "deal lists" and used to calculate how much you have profited from your cultivation. Your profit is used against you at court appearances and can result in higher fines for smaller growers, and longer terms of imprisonment for larger producers. If you are subject to asset seizures these lists will be used to increase the amount you must pay.

Avoiding Detection of Odour and Heat

The distinctive odour that cannabis plants produce when they're growing can easily be contained within the growing area. The smell will not permeate through walls. However, vents can be a concern, so try to position your ventilation ducts so that they do not allow odours to be detected.

Place filters over the vents to prevent any pungent smells from escaping. Carbon filters work well. However, although the activated charcoal can last up to 12 months, you should replace them much earlier. Ionisers have some effect on controlling odours in smaller setups, and work by emitting negative ions into the grow area. Air purifiers that combine powerful ion emissions with multi-stage, odour absorbing carbon filters can be purchased and are ideal for smaller grow rooms. Ozone generators can also be used to remove odours from your grow area and they are effective; however, many growers avoid them due to the health risk that ozone (O_3) can pose. Ozone molecules quickly break down once released; typically within 30 seconds, however, once the odours have been destroyed O_3 can easily build up in the room. You can build an ozone generator yourself using a high voltage neon sign transformer, but ensure that you place this near an external exhaust fan and only consider using one when other methods prove to be ineffective. I was convicted of running a warehouse-sized cannabis factory that was located in the heart of a residential area for over two years and there was never any smell detected. All we did was install carbon filters over the exhaust fans and replace them regularly.

Police forces now have helicopters equipped with thermal imaging cameras that identify unusual sources of heat. When flown over grow room locations, they can cause problems for the cultivator; however, they are not as effective when used in daylight hours and anyone running a larger setup should have the light cycle adjusted to take advantage of this. Locate larger farms in industrial areas where manufacturing occurs or, alternatively, cultivate in rural areas where flights don't take place. Smaller cultivators need not worry about heat sources unless the grow room is located in a loft space, as the imager is not that sensitive. The authorities don't like to release figures but the percentage of grow rooms detected by thermal imaging cameras is small. The majority of seizures are made by police acting on information from informants.

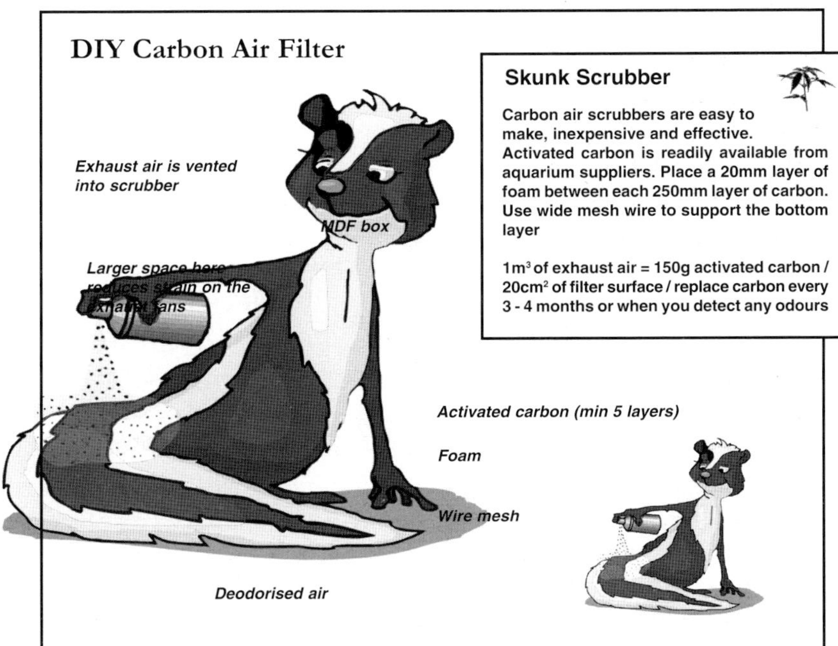

Skunk Scrubber

Carbon air scrubbers are easy to make, inexpensive and effective. Activated carbon is readily available from aquarium suppliers. Place a 20mm layer of foam between each 250mm layer of carbon. Use wide mesh wire to support the bottom layer

1m³ of exhaust air = 150g activated carbon / 20cm² of filter surface / replace carbon every 3 - 4 months or when you detect any odours

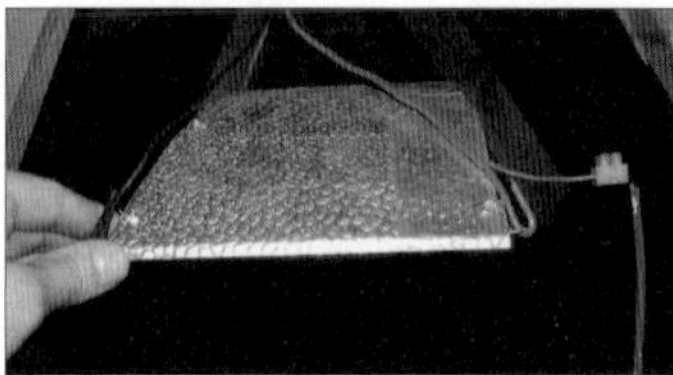

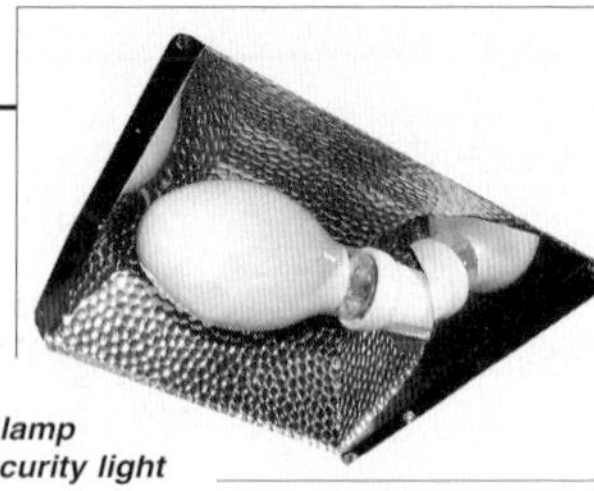

70-watt HPS grow lamp converted from security light

DIY Growlamps

400-watt Industrial Lowbay lights are around £50 +VAT, come in MH or HPS and can be adapted to suit any garden. This has one end cut off and the ballast remoted outside the grow cabinet. Many growers leave the casing intact. Ballasts can be remoted up to 2.5m. The bulb holder can also be mounted on the ends

Growers can run up to 1000-watts per bedroom without raising suspicion i.e. 2 bedroom house = 2000W

The ballast has been removed from this Lowbay casing and mounted away from the lamp in a vented enclosure

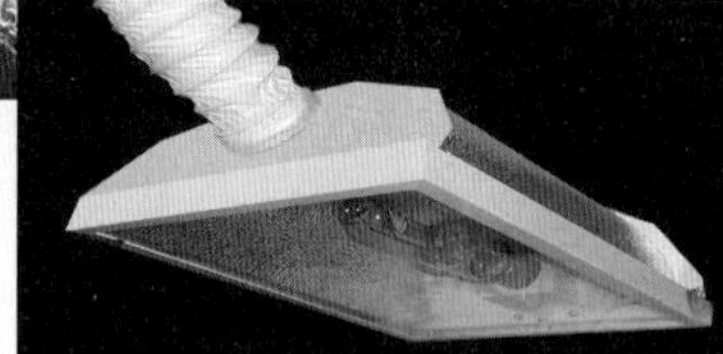

This air-cooled lamp cost over £200 and still needed an inline fan. You can build a 400-watt version for a fraction of the cost using a Lowbay. Remote the ballast and fit ducting to the lamp. Air is drawn over the bulb and ducted away using an inline fan

Fluorescent tubes mounted in a reflector

Air-cooled 400-watt lowbay light has a vent mounted over a hole cut into the casing. An inline fan draws air through the lamp.

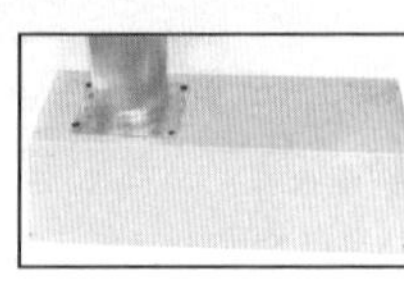

Chapter 4

LIGHTING

Stolen sweets are best. Cibber, 1671–1757

Electricity companies monitor their customers' bills and if there is a sharp rise in consumption they will contact you, usually quite innocently, to ask why. They may even want to check to see if the meter is faulty, which should be avoided. Smaller setups using fluorescent lights, or small high-pressure sodium's, will not make a marked impression on consumption, but a larger rotation setup with six-plus, 1000-watt sodium's will spin the meter dials.

Some enterprising outlaws bypass their electricity meters so that a false reading is given to the electric company. Others have been known to attach modified transformers, known as *black boxes,* to the outside two cables entering the meter box, causing the dials to spin backwards. Companies are aware of these moves and are bringing out ever more sophisticated systems, but even digital card and key meters can be bypassed. These frauds will increase the severity of any punishment, should your grow room be found, and are definitely not recommended for amateur electricians.

Electricity can kill you if you don't know what you are doing!

The combination of electricity and water that you find in grow room environments is potentially lethal, so mount all fittings off the floor and away from water storage tanks. Install circuit breakers into your setup to shut the system down if you develop a problem. If you are unsure about any wiring, consult a qualified electrician. Growers in some locations run their lights from generators and, providing you have a back up in case of power failure, they can work well. Even silent running units are audible though, but it's possible to muffle generators by enclosing them in a soundproof box. Using a generator to supplement the mains supply is a good system to opt for. Approximate electricity cost per day of horticultural lights, priced in both Sterling (£) / Euros (€) - averaged on UK rates are:

Lamp	Vegetative	Flowering
400w	£0.55 /€0.90	£0.40 /€0.65
600w	£0.80 /€1.30	£0.55 /€0.90
1000w	£1.25 /€2.00	£0.85 /€1.40

With careful management, it is possible to run a grow room that doesn't attract the curiosity of the electric company. When setting up a unit in a new location it's useful to have bills from the previous 12 months – they allow you to mirror the readings.

Light is one of the major factors that will affect cannabis plant growth. Plants use a process known as ***photosynthesis*** to convert carbon dioxide into sugar, releasing oxygen back into the atmosphere, as they carry out this chemical process. We can't see all of the light wavelengths used in photosynthesis; although light appears white to the human eye, it is in fact a mixture of colours. Plants absorb the red, violet and blue spectrum, leaving green as the colour we see, indicating that green is the least absorbed of the colour spectrum. Lamps are usually rated in Watts and lumens, however; this is not as accurate as the standard measure of energy known as Photosynthetic Available Radiation (PAR).

Photosynthetic Available Radiation (PAR)

This differs from lumens in that it is not a direct measure of energy. It is the standard measure of light available for photosynthesis and is expressed in photons. Photosynthesis takes place as plants absorb these photons. PAR measures lamp output between 400 and 700 nm (nanometers).

Watt (W)
This is the standard unit of power. 1 joule of energy per second corresponds to a power of 1-watt. As a general guide, cannabis gardens require at least 50-watts of HID light per $30cm^2$.

Lumens
Lumens are the measure of light intensity and are relative to, but different from wattage and based on what the human eye can see; rather than what a plant uses, for photosynthesis. Indoor cannabis gardens require between 3,000 and 9,000 lumens per $30cm^2$. Successful gardens receive at least 6,000 lumens per $30cm^2$. Lumen output is a measure of *flux*, (light energy that a lamp emits). This peaks at around 550 nanometers (nm), which is the green region of the light spectrum, and decreases at both the red and blue wavelengths. This means that two light sources emitting the same total amount of energy can have different lumen ratings.

Lux
This is a measure of *illumination* and refers to the light energy that reaches your growing surface. Lux is equivalent to lumens/m^2, but also takes into account reflector efficiency, glass barriers and your lamps distance from the plants.

Colour temperature
Higher colour temperature means more blue colour, lower temperature means more red. Colour temperature is expressed in **degrees Kelvin**.

Colour rendering index (CRI)
CRI measures how true to colour that a light source makes an object appear. A perfect light source would have a CRI of 100. In general, the higher the CRI rating of a lamp, the better the colours show.

This can all become confusing so simply ensure you use a minimum of 50 W of HID per $30cm^2$. The more light that cannabis receives, the better it will grow, especially if you are releasing carbon dioxide (CO_2) into the room. However, heat build up can become a problem so ensure your room (or lamps) are well ventilated. Even under 1000-watt HID lamps, plants only receive 25% of the light available outside on a sunny day. Cannabis that is grown in low light levels will be tall with thin stems and sparse flowers. Lamps are hung as close as possible to the tops of your plants without scorching them: typically at about 45cm with HID lamps. Test the temperature with the back of your hand, it should not feel uncomfortably hot.

The two main types of lights used for successful indoor cultivation are fluorescents and high intensity discharge (HID) lamps. Mercury vapour (MV) lamps can be used to cultivate cannabis plants but are extremely inefficient, producing only 8000 lumens per 175-watts. In comparison, a high-pressure sodium lamp will emit 15,000 lumens per 150-watts. Plant growth is also slower under MV lamps due to the colour spectrum they emit, which is poor compared to other lights that are available. Don't use halogen lamps to grow cannabis, in theory the PAR is good but they induce huge internode spacing, poor vegetative growth, and produce dangerous amounts of heat.

Fluorescent Lighting

Fluorescent lights are used primarily for growing cuttings or in small closet-type setups. They have reduced output compared to HID lights, but they are cheap to run. When using fluorescents in enclosed setups you must bear in mind that the heat to light ratio is higher than most metal halide lamps and that although they can be used for some mini and micro installations, they are not recommended.

When using fluorescents use the *cool white* variety, which are rich in the blue spectrum of light and will produce bushy plants up to 38cm high. They can be purchased from electrical wholesalers and retail outlets. It is relatively straightforward to build a system with several tubes attached to a plywood base that has been covered in reflective foil. Alternatively, the grower can purchase ready-made fluorescent modules that come housed in their own reflectors.

Fluorescents marketed as grow lights are available but are much less efficient than standard fluorescents and produce less light. High output fluorescent tubes are available in 60 and 122cm lengths that give out a maximum of 24,000 lumens; however, they cost as much as high intensity discharge lamps, which are a better option.

Many cultivators make use of fluorescents as a low-cost addition to HID systems, using them to supplement the light supply. Fluorescents can be suspended above crops or hung between individual plants to boost growth.

High Intensity Discharge Lamps (HID)
HID lamps are the main choice of the indoor cannabis cultivator. They are cheap and efficient to run and provide the necessary light spectrum. Each light requires a ballast that comes ready-wired as a remote unit, with the light and reflector connected to it. In some Dutch lights the ballast is built into the light casing and these Poot lamps are the main choice for commercial nurseries that supply garden plants to the trade. Lamps are hung in rows above the greenhouse crops.

Metal Halides (MH)
Metal halides (MH) produce a natural-looking light and are used by some cultivators during the vegetative growth phase. Once flowering is induced, the lights are replaced with high-pressure sodiums that are better suited for flowering. This is unnecessary as plants will grow efficiently under sodium lights for both the vegetative and flowering stages, and furthermore, the plants will have a shorter internodal length. MH lights are available in 175w, 200w, 400w and 1,000-watt sizes. The low wattage lamps are recommended when raising cuttings.

High Pressure Sodium (HPS)
HPS lights are more efficient than MH lamps, producing more light and less heat per Watt of electricity consumed. The light produced is from the correct spectrum for flowering and still gives good results during the growth phase. Sodium lights are deficient in the blue spectrum and are therefore not used for raising cuttings, although this can be compensated for by adding fluorescents to the garden.

The concentration of red and yellow light that HPS emit promotes a higher flower-to-leaf ratio in growing plants than MH or fluorescents. HPS lights are available in 75w, 100w, 110w, 125w, 400w, 600w and 1,000-watt sizes. They can also be adapted from security lights: as long as they are high-pressure sodium, they are suitable for cultivating.

Son-T-Agro

Son-T-Agro lamps are HPS lamps available commercially for horticultural use. The manufacturers have added 30% more light in the blue spectrum to the bulb. They have a slight increase in output over standard HPS (typically around 6%) but have a 25% shorter life. You can buy lamps in the standard 250w to 1,000-watt range. If you already use HPS lamps you can purchase the Son-T-Agro bulbs separately and they will be compatible with your system.

Light Movers

The most efficient way to use high intensity discharge lamps is to keep them moving within the grow room. Moving the lamps ensures an even distribution of light over the crop, eliminates uneven growth patterns, and produces a more uniform and consistent crop. Because they are moving, the lights can be lowered closer to the plants without burning the leaves, thus promoting faster growth and higher yields. The light also covers a larger area, saving on the cost of additional lamps and electricity. There are two types of light movers available to indoor cultivators.

Linear Movers

These movers carry the light unit back and forth over a 2-metre, straight rail. A 30-second delay is applied at either end to ensure maximum coverage. Linear movers increase the effective growing area and are both easy to install and cheap to run, using only 5-watts of electricity. Linear movers are ideal for narrow growing areas.

Circular Movers

They are less efficient than linear movers; the 360° movement can result in lower light levels towards the centre and edges of the growing area. However, growers have reported using these setups to increase yields in grow rooms where the plants cover the complete floor space. Three-arm movers are the most effective but if possible, try to avoid circular movers and opt for a linear light rail unit.

Reflectors

High-pressure sodium lights are sold as complete units with a ballast and a shade, called a reflector. The type of reflector your lamp has will be determined by the price you pay. There are two basic types: open-ended and closed. The open-ended reflector allows heat to escape and can be mounted closer to the plants, while closed reflectors are more suited to light rails. Aluminium mirror polish is the standard finish for most reflectors and is adequate for indoor cultivation. More efficient systems have a highly reflective *anocoil* insert. This dimpled surface reflects approximately 10% more light from the bulb than other reflectors at the same mounting height.

Air-cooled reflectors are also available and are ideal for small areas where heat build-up is a problem. These reflectors are sealed units with a toughened glass shield that allows the light to pass through but retains the heat. The excess heat is drawn out through 10cm ducting using an extractor fan and dispersed. You can improvise your own air-cooled lamps by placing a sheet of glass between the light and your enclosed plants (see *p85*).

Timers

HID lights use high inductive currents when starting up. Most timers will burn out under this surge, leaving your lights permanently on, so it is important to use a heavy-duty timer when controlling the day length in a grow room.

Contactors, which are heavy load relays, can be wired to start either individual or groups of lights. The contactor removes the load from the timer and is easy to install. If you are unsure of the wiring, consult an electrician. A qualified electrician can wire a contactor to a four-gang extension lead for you without knowing its use. Choose a three-pole, 28-amp inductive, 75-amp resistive contactor if you intend to use four 600w or two 1,000w lamps. Alternatively, ready-made kits are available from most hydroponic retailers.

Ventilation

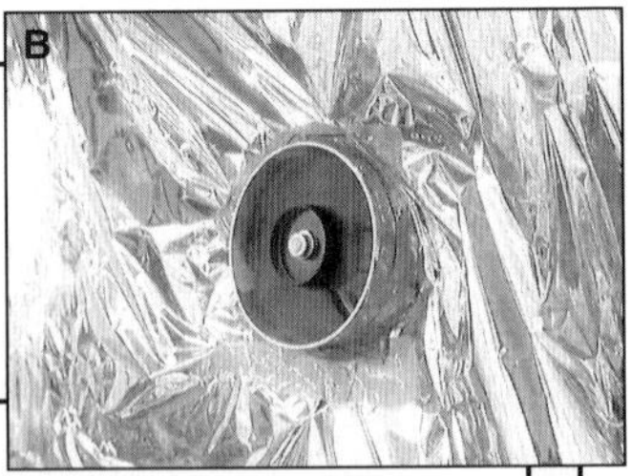

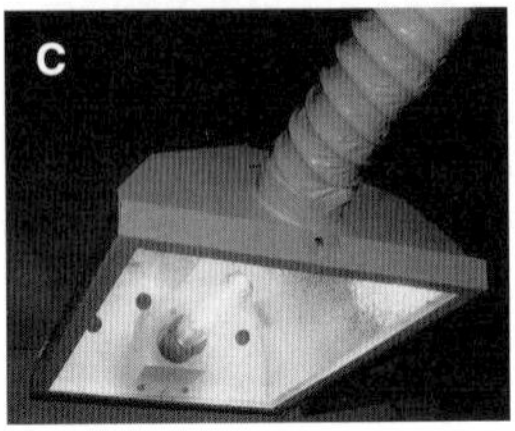

How to determine fan size in cubic metres/hour

Calculate the volume of the grow area you intend to ventilate.
This is done by multiplying:

Length × Width × Height = Volume of your room in cubic metres (m^3)

Air should be replaced every 3 minutes/ **20** x per hour.
Therefore, multiply the volume of your growroom by **20**

For example, a room:

2 m × 2 m × 2.5 m high = 10m^3

10m^3 × 20 changes per hour = 200m^3 *per hour fan*

install a 225m^3 fan (or a combination of smaller fans equal to 225m^3) to be on the safe side

(A) 225m^3 silent, inline fan
(B) Air intake fan in an enclosed grow
(C) Air-cooled lamps remove heat directly from source
(D) Office desk fans are ideal for air circulation in grow areas

Chapter 5

HEAT, AIR and CO_2

Behold, the bush burned with fire. Exodus III. 2

Daytime temperature within your grow space, without adding supplemental CO_2 should be **21-26.5°C**. If you are adding CO_2 then it can rise to between **26.5-32°C**. In the last two weeks of flowering the daytime temperature should be kept between **21-26.5°C** and CO_2 reduced to adjust for the plants lower metabolism. Night temperatures should be kept above **15°C** to prevent stress, stimulate hormones and reduce stem elongation. Temperature can be measured using a maximum and minimum thermometer; it will indicate the extremes of temperatures reached. Water and nutrient solution should be heated in their storage tanks to around **23°C**. Use an aquarium heater, they are inexpensive and available at aquarium suppliers

Due to the heat given off by HID lighting systems, it is unlikely that you will ever need to heat a grow room during the daylight cycle. During night time cold spells, however, a thermostatically controlled air-blowing heater will maintain the temperature. Fan heaters designed for greenhouse use work well. During the summer months your main problem will be reducing the temperature to manageable levels. Portable air-conditioning units can be purchased second-hand to keep grow rooms cool, and venting the room will also assist by removing warm air and maintaining good air circulation. Use office desk fans to create air circulation. Suspend the fans upside down from the ceiling or place them on prepared ledges. Alternatively, you can buy fans that come with their own stands. Circulation is important within the grow room to distribute carbon dioxide supplies evenly, and also to keep odours and temperatures down. The plants need to sway gently in the fan breeze, a movement that helps to strengthen their stems. Larger setups need horticultural fans that are mounted high in the room.

Humidity

Humidity is the water vapour content of air, and is measured in percentages using a hygrometer that should be positioned on the grow room wall. Humidity during vegetative growth can be kept at an even 50%, but during flowering it should be reduced to between 30% and 40% to ensure that *Botrytis,* or mould, does not attack the buds. Humidity and air temperature are relative: warm air holds more water vapour, thereby lowering humidity levels, while cool air holds less water vapour and therefore raises the level of humidity. It's unlikely that humidity levels will ever be too low in a grow room environment due to plant transpiration and the amounts of water used. Using a dehumidifier easily controls high humidity levels.

Carbon Dioxide (CO_2)

Carbon dioxide is essential for plant growth. The atmosphere contains about 350 parts per million (ppm); however, plants can tolerate greater levels of CO_2 than are naturally available. In the early stages of plant evolution the earth's atmosphere had much higher concentrations of CO_2 and plants have not lost the ability to utilize it. By increasing the level of CO_2 in your grow room to around 1,000 ppm you can expect an increase in yield of approximately 25%. This level is the most cost-effective but can be increased by a further 500 ppm with a corresponding increase in yield.

The most common method of supplying CO_2 to grow rooms is with cylinders. You can rent cylinders from welding supply companies or borrow them from bar owners, who use them to pump beer. Hydroponics suppliers stock valves and timers that are screwed into the cylinders and adjusted to inject the atmosphere with gas. There are controllers on the market that you simply program with the size of you're grow room and the ppm you require: the valve then opens automatically. Plants do not need CO_2 during the night cycle, so the equipment is off during this time.

To determine the amount of CO_2 your room requires, first calculate the area of your grow room in cubic centimetres (length x breadth x height). The CO_2 levels will naturally be around 300 ppm so to take levels up to the optimum of 1500 ppm you will need to raise it by 1200 ppm. Multiply your room volume by 0.0012 to give you the amount of carbon dioxide needed in cubic cm. Smaller plants that have just been started will need a third less CO_2 so set your regulator to inject the required amount every hour. Use a CO_2 testing kit to check that the grow room levels are correct and, if necessary, adjust your delivery. When using carbon dioxide it is better to have a closed system that doesn't vent the room to the outside to ensure you don't waste any of the gas. Temperature is controlled by air conditioners set to re-circulate.

Alternative supplies of CO_2 can be generated with growth gas heaters that burn propane gas to emit atmospheric carbon dioxide. While gas heaters can be useful in winter months, they give off too much heat for most indoor setups. You can supply smaller crops with CO_2 using other methods that don't allow you to accurately control the levels of gas, but that give higher readings. One method is to make a 2 litre solution of sugar , warm water and a brewer's yeast tablet, available at home brew suppliers. Place the open bottle into the grow cabinet and replace weekly. As it ferments the solution will produce half the volume of sugar consumed as gas. Another method is to add vinegar or lemon juice to sodium bicarbonate (baking soda), which causes it to froth up and release CO_2. Mix a small amount in a container and then place it into your cabinet and close the doors. Small cabinets only need a teaspoon of baking soda, but you need to do this on a regular basis.

CO_2 is comprised of carbon and oxygen. Plants use most of the carbon and exhale the oxygen. The carbon is combined with nutrients and water to produce phosphatides and sugar. Liquid carbon can be added to the nutrient solution instead of using CO_2 gas supplementation, which can be useful, especially during the flowering stage. However, it means changing the nutrient solution every three days, which is not cost effective for larger grow operations. There are also problems associated with pH levels and growers are advised to use hydrogen peroxide (H_2O_2) in the nutrient solution, added on a daily basis, to keep down anaerobic bacteria and fungi. Liquid carbon is not suitable for re-circulating or organic setups and its use is still controversial. Some growers maintain that it is ineffective.

Dry ice gives off CO_2 as it melts. If you have access to a regular supply of dry ice you can use it, although it's an inefficient way of delivering the gas. Dry ice is frozen carbon dioxide that degrades at around 10% per day in a freezer. In the heat of a grow room it melts rapidly, delivering excessive levels of CO_2. While the excessive levels aren't harmful, they are a waste of the gas.

Carbon dioxide supplementation increases yields but is time-consuming and unnecessary for good results. Some growers report that high levels of CO_2 in the flowering room at, or approaching, harvest time can actually lower the potency of your crop. It's better to stop feeding the gas 10 days before you harvest. There are security implications when moving large tanks into and out of your growing location. An alternative is to ensure the plants have a good supply of fresh air drawn in from outside the grow room, providing the plants with CO_2 at between 300 and 350 ppm during daylight hours. Filter the ducts with nylon stockings to keep out insects.

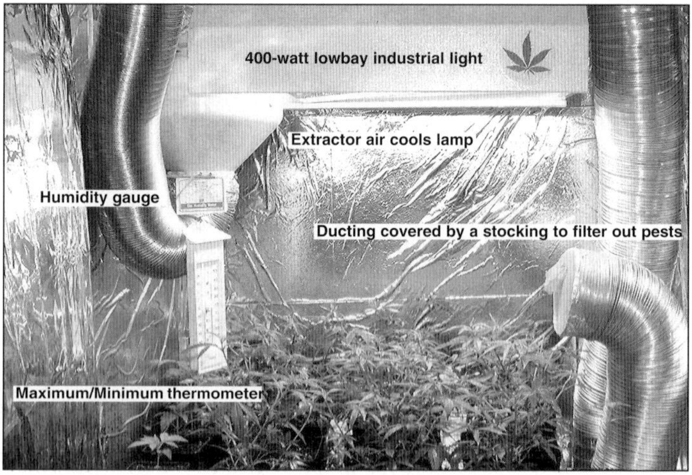

Chapter 6

CHOOSING PLANTS

The fruits of the spirit. The Litany

It is important to select a variety of cannabis that is well suited to indoor cultivation. Seeds from imported African, Colombian or Jamaican weed are unsuitable for cultivation in the cooler regions of Europe, even under horticultural lights. Quality seeds can be purchased by mail order from suppliers in Holland, The UK or Canada, and some companies specialize in *feminised* seeds that will produce all female crops (see *Breeding*). The seeds are generally of a consistent quality and arrive in plain packaging through the mail. Some Dutch companies won't send seeds to Germany, France or addresses outside Europe, but there are other companies that will. Alternatively, go and collect the seeds yourself.

Most growers choose *Cannabis indica* varieties for their indoor crops. Pure *Cannabis sativas* grow too tall. Outdoor skunk growers also opt for indicas, but there are sativa hybrids available that perform well. Remember that these seeds will be the basis of your future stock and mother plants for several generations, so choose carefully. Most varieties of *Cannabis indica* are easy to cultivate but novice growers should avoid some of the "Big Bud" varieties, as they are notoriously difficult to clone.

Seeds should be small, brown and speckled. Lighter colour seeds will not be mature enough to germinate. Store your seeds at low temperatures in sealed jars to keep them viable for a longer period by slowing down the rate of respiration. Fresh seeds will have a 90% germination rate but this dramatically reduces over time. After three to four years the germination rate will have dropped to about 20%.

Dormant seeds need to be made up of an average of 20% water so store them away from heat sources.

Yields

The following crop weights are intended as guidelines only. Plant yields are dependent on several important factors such as variety, light levels, environmental conditions, time of harvest, and cultivation techniques. For example, using intensive rotation – such as the Dutch Sea Of Green (SOG) – it is possible to produce a crop of high quality cannabis buds every two weeks. However, the yield will be lower than with plants given a longer vegetative growth period. Yields from SOG plants grown with 15cm between individual plant stalks, in rotation, can average between:

10 and 14-grams (dried buds per plant)

Other cultivators prefer to concentrate on individual high-yielding plants. Grown for longer periods in higher light levels, and using techniques like defoliation and secondary budding, these crops can yield more than:

250-grams (dried buds per plant)

A *Cannabis indica* variety such as a *Shiva Shanti*, grown under a HPS lamp and receiving 6,000 lumens, with optimum environmental conditions, and flowered at a height of 40cm for 55 days, should produce:

150 to 125-grams (dried buds per plant)

However, most indoor cultivators are happy to harvest between:

50 and 60-grams (from plants grown in optimum conditions)

The Screen of Green (SCROG) technique allows growers to cultivate crops that utilize more of the lumens emitted from their lamps. Micro and mini systems can be built to take advantage of this by using low wattage lamps. A 100-watt HPS over a single plant, in an enclosed grow unit, will yield:

20-grams (dried buds per plant)

The plant density in SCROG is less than with other systems, which is a benefit should the crop be discovered by the authorities. Using a 600-watt HPS over a single plant results in yields that can be more than:

70-grams (dried buds per plant)

Outdoor cultivators can expect high yields from mature plants, but this depends on the growing conditions during the season. Cannabis plants do not require constant direct sunlight. As long as they receive about five hours daily and have more than a 1metre^2 growing space, *Cannabis ruderalis* varieties can yield up to:

300-grams (dried buds per plant)

Cannabis indicas can produce yields of up to:

500-grams (dried buds per plant)

Cannabis sativa varieties, in optimum conditions, can yield well over:

1 kilo (dried buds per plant)

You need to decide if the crop is going to be grown organically or hydroponically before choosing a particular production method. Both methods are suitable for indoor cannabis production.

Providing optimum growing conditions ensures your chosen variety reaches it's full genetic potential. Ensure air, water, nutrients, and light are supplied within the correct balance and temperature range. If any of these drop below optimum in your grow room the complex growth chain breaks down and your yield suffers

(A) The notorious London Cabbie shows how it's done

A

Organics

Organic crops are grown without any pesticides or chemical fertilizers. Hydroponic crops can still be grown organically using organic feed. These can be purchased or made from 'Teas' . Don't use manure and if you are using hydro-organics (Bioponics). Strain and filter the tea to avoid blocking your system.

Organic fertilizers

Alfalfa Pellets *(NPK 3-1-2)* 120g/m^2
Blood meal *(NPK 12-0-0)* 30g/m^2
Bone meal *(NPK 2-11-0)* 75g/m^2
B&Q multi-organic *(NPK 4-4-4)* 70g/m^2
Corn Gluten *(NPK 6-0-0)* 45g/m^2
Poultry manure *(NPK 4-3-2.5)* 75g/m^2
Fish emulsion *(NPK 5-2-2 liquid)* 5ml/m^2
Kelp *(NPK 1-0.2-2)* 45g/m^3
Insect manure *(NPK 4-3-2)* 105g/m^2
Soybean meal *(NPK 6-1.5-2)* 60g/m^2

Guano has variable nutrient content but is safe. Other fresh manures (including poultry) must be well composted before use. Never use fresh or raw manure, especially during flowering.

B

(B) Organic plants at Mr. Nice Seedbank Switzerland

Teas are made by hanging a stocking containing your organic fertilizer in a bucket of water

Organic crops are free from any chemical residue that can remain in the plant tissue after harvest

Nitrates and other agents used in chemical fertilizers are harmful to smoke

(A) This organic Hindu Kush in a perlite compost mix is watered with bottled mineral water and only lightly fed with organic tea.

Chapter 7

ORGANIC CROPS

Earth laughs in flowers. Hamatreya

Organic cultivation in its purest form means using no chemical fertilizer or pesticides on your crop. It is possible to achieve good results organically; however, most cultivators refer to crops grown in soils or potting composts as "organic" despite the fact that chemicals are used. You can achieve more consistent results by using controlled doses of soluble fertilizer, but you must be careful.

Organic-based systems have advantages over hydroponic setups. Inexperienced growers find soil, or compost-based cultivation, more forgiving as the medium provides a natural buffer for pH levels. Smaller scale growers can save on their start-up costs by building organic systems that require far less equipment than hydroponic setups. Many commercial cultivators still grow organically, even in large-scale farms. There are growers who claim that organically produced buds smoke and taste better than hydroponic crops, but there is no real evidence to support this theory. It is virtually impossible to distinguish between the two, especially if the hydroponic crop has been fed fresh pH-adjusted water prior to harvesting in order to flush out any chemical residue.

Take care when selecting the type of soil to use in potting mixes. Ordinary topsoil, unlike commercially available potting composts, is not sterilized and can contain harmful organisms and insect larvae. Topsoil dries out far too quickly for use in pots or containers and has variable nutrient contents. It's advisable to purchase a good quality potting compost to cultivate your crop. If this is not available it is possible to make your own.

Compost

Compost is made from organic materials. The best compost is manure, which contains organic material that has been ingested, digested and broken down by animals.

Making your own compost

You can make compost yourself by building a compost heap and allowing vegetable material, grass trimmings, and other organic waste to decompose. Providing air, nitrogen and water will assist the microbes in carrying out the decomposition.

Air

Start your heap with a base of bricks or blocks to vent and raise it. Place thin sticks and branches on top of the bricks or blocks before adding 25cm of organic matter. (You can create chimneys that provide air to the heap by inserting posts into the stack and then removing them later.) The side of your compost heap should be vertical, supported by blocks or wooden slats.

Nitrogen

On top of the first 25cm layer of organic matter add either manure, horticultural nitrogen fertilizer, or dried blood to provide nitrogen. Alternate with lime every other layer.

Water

Try to keep the heap moist but not saturated. Add water to the heap if the contents dry out. Once the organisms begin to break down the vegetable matter in the compost heap, they generate a lot of heat. The heat kills off all the weed seeds and undesirable organisms so once this process starts, cover the top of the heap to contain it.

After six weeks, turn the compost with a garden fork to ensure that it is well mixed. After a further six weeks the compost will be ready and can be blended with peat and sand to produce a good quality potting compost.

Some of the best commercially available potting composts are loam-based. Loam can be made by cutting out sections of grass turf and stacking the sections top side down. Build your stack one metre high and place compost between each layer. The loam will take 12 months to form and will require sterilizing. This is best done outside by heating a large drum of water and passing the steam through the loam, which is placed in a perforated container above it. Alternatively, pour a 5% bleach solution through the loam. Small amounts can be sterilized in an oven or microwave where the loam should be heated until steam is given off.

Preparing Your Potting Mix

Ingredients:
7 parts sterilized loam or organic compost
(Mix the compost with equal amounts of soft sand before use)
3 parts sterilized sphagnum moss peat.
(Add four parts if using compost)
2 parts soft sand
(even with organic compost that already has sand in)

To each 25kg mix add 100-grams of *base fertilizer* and 25-grams lime:

A good base fertilizer is composed of:
1 part sulphate of potash
2 parts bone meal (see *p109*)
2 parts superphosphate of lime

Once you have mixed your potting compost it is advisable to check the pH level, which is a measure of the soil's acidity. Organic cannabis grows best at levels of around 6.5, with 6 and 7 being acceptable extremes. The pH level can be tested with a probe that is inserted into the soil or with a chemical testing kit. Both are available at stores.

Commercially available potting composts do not need pH adjusting and are already sterilized. Choose a loam-based mixture. If this is not available, a general purpose potting compost will produce good results. Tomatoes have similar nutritional requirements to cannabis so any compost mixes designed specifically for their cultivation are ideal, including growbags.

To raise pH levels add small amounts of ground lime
To lower pH levels add acid peat or sulphate of ammonia

To improve the water-holding ability of the potting compost add perlite to the mix. Perlite is a naturally occurring mineral that is commercially available for horticultural use. Perlite improves drainage, and at the same time has good moisture-holding ability and absorbs nutrients, preventing them from flushing out of the soil.

Add 1 part perlite to 1 part potting compost (50% mix)

Cannabis prefers free draining soil that supplies the roots with oxygen.

Pot and Container Sizes

15cm square plastic pots are ideal for most indoor cultivation techniques. Square pots allow you to pack the plants tightly together during the early stages of development, in order to make the most use of the available light. If these aren't available, any container larger than 15cm is adequate, providing it has drainage holes in its base. Plastic tomato cultivation pots are cheap and readily available. They are suitable for hydroponic pot culture, which requires 5 to 10 litre capacities, but they are on the large side for rotation cropping. Pots over 30cm are too big for serious indoor organic cultivation.

Growbags are plastic sleeves that are pre-packed with potting compost. They can hold between one and three plants. Insert an 8cm pot through a hole in the polythene to make watering easier. Cutting drainage slits in the base of the bag will prevent water logging. Some growers purchase potting compost in plastic bags and simply flatten them, cut slits into the top, and use them as growbags.

You can use plastic bags to grow plants in if nothing else is available. Alternatively, packs of ready-made cultivation bags are available from horticultural suppliers. Outdoor growers can use thick bin liners or rubbish bags. The first outdoor crop I ever grew was in bags, as I couldn't afford any pots. The bags still yielded around 350-grams per plant. All pots and containers used indoors should stand in saucers or waterproof trays. You can purchase them in various sizes or make them from builder's polythene fixed to a wooden frame. Children's paddling pools can be used as trays for some indoor cultivation techniques.

(A) Peat pellets are soaked in rain or mineral water before use and can be used for organic cuttings and seeds

(B) This plant was started in a rockwool hydroponic setup and later transferred to an organic growbag

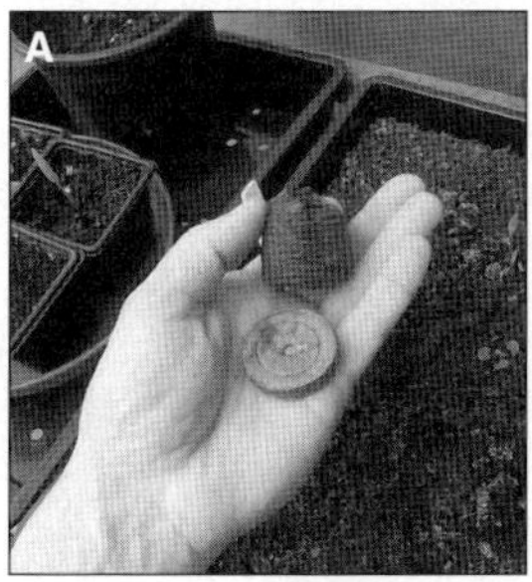

(C) Bonsai mother plant in 15cm square pot. This plant provides a small number of organic cuttings every 2 weeks. Twice a year the rootball is removed from the pot and 2.5cm is cut from the sides and base. The plant is placed back into the pot and fresh compost is added to fill the trimmed edges

Clones have just been misted so appear drooped

(A) Clones rooted in rockwool
(B) Young female clone
(C) Clones started in hydro setup
(D) Organic plant from same cuttings (C)

Does the Moon influences cannabis planting?

The moon has 4 Phases or quarters (lasting about 7 days each). The first 2 quarters are during the waxing (increasing light) between the New and the Full moon. The third and fourth quarters are after the full moon when the light is waning. Planting by the moon is an ancient tradition but scientific research validates it. The Earth is in a large gravitational field, influenced by both the sun and moon. The tides are highest at the time of the New and the Full moon, when sun and moon are lined up with Earth. Just as the moon pulls the tides in oceans, it pulls moisture in the earth causing it to rise and encouraging germination and growth

Soil moisture content is highest at the time of the Full moon and seeds absorb more water at this time...

Chapter 8

STARTING A CROP

Necessity hath no law. Speech 1664

From Seed

When germinated, cannabis seeds will be approximately 50% male, 50% female, unless you are using feminised seeds (see *Breeding*). It is possible to increase the female-to-male ratio by treating the seeds with chemicals before germinating.

Ethylene, a naturally occurring gas given off by ripening bananas, has been found to increase the feminisation of seeds. Before germination, place the seeds in a sealed plastic bag containing banana peels for 14 days. Wrap the skins in tissue to absorb any moisture they give off. Keep the bag in a warm place and air the seeds regularly, replacing the skins as they ripen.

Oestrogen, found in birth control pills, has a similar effect. Dissolve 1 pill in 50ml of water, and then soak your seeds in this solution overnight. Sprout the seeds on tissue paper saturated with the same solution.

Sensa Soak is marketed in the Netherlands as a commercial seed feminiser and is used as a soak before germination.

Increases of between 10 and 25% more females have been achieved using these methods. For best results, germinate untreated seeds in vermiculite soaked in a weak solution of hydroponic feed, which has been diluted by at least 50%. Place the vermiculite in a shallow tray or container (aluminium foil is suitable) and pour in nutrient solution until it is saturated. Plant the seeds just below the surface about the depth of the seed, ensuring that they are lightly covered. It is not necessary to place them in a darkened area. Instead, leave the tray exposed to at least 18 hours of uninterrupted daylight and keep the vermiculite moist. The temperature should not exceed 26°C. This method of germination can be used for organic plants but for true organic gardening you should start them in a 'seed' potting compost, or a proprietary soil less compost. They will only require fresh water instead of a dilute feed.

Within one to seven days the seeds will begin germination. The first stage is the absorption of water, followed closely by the emergence of the ***radicle*** or root. As the radicle forces its way downward the ***hypocotyl*** or stem extends toward the light, still covered by the seed case. As the ***cotyledon,*** or first leaves, enlarge they shed the seed husk, allowing the first true leaves to emerge. Don't be tempted to pull off the seed casing as you can damage the hypocotyl. As soon as the seedlings are between 2 and 3cm tall, remove them carefully from the vermiculite and plant them into pots, cubes or polystyrene cups, ensuring that they are well watered. They are now ready to be placed into the nursery or vegetative growing area.

Damping Off

Damping off is a fungal infection that kills seedlings. The base of the stem rots and the plant falls over and dies. Some growers spray seedlings with a diluted, preventative systemic fungicide as a precaution. It's not essential to spray, just ensure that you give the seedlings the best possible start by cleaning all your equipment thoroughly before use, and by using fresh water (or weak nutrient solution) to feed them. Low light levels; low temperatures, high humidity and waterlogged medium all contribute to damping off.

Cloning

Cloning is simply taking cuttings from a mature plant. It ensures that you have a 100% female crop. Plants that are in flower are difficult to clone so females are identified through the flowering of test cuttings. Cuttings are taken from the plants while they are in the vegetative state, and then carefully labelled. These cuttings are then rooted and flowered. It is also possible to induce cannabis to flower and then, as soon as the females are identified, place them back under 24 hours of continuous light, forcing them to revert to the vegetative cycle. However, this process can be time consuming and most growers prefer to use cuttings. Female cannabis plants can be cloned as soon as they have developed healthy side shoots. The older the plant, the more shoots you will have.

Once you have a healthy mature female plant that shows signs of vigorous growth you can make genetically identical copies of her that will exhibit exactly the same traits. Start by cutting young growth tips, about 8 to 10cm long, from the mother plant. Use a sharp, sterilized pair of scissors. Most horticultural guides will tell you that scissors pinch and damage the stem tissue but that doesn't affect the strike rate of young cuttings and scissors are easier to use than razors. Cut the stem at a slight angle to expose a larger area, and then dip the stalk into a rooting gel. Gels are available from all good gardening retailers and are better than rooting powders. Place the rooting gel you are working with in a separate container to avoid cross contamination of any possible infections. Remove any large leaves and place the cutting stem 2 to 3cm into the rooting medium.

If you are gardening organically you can use *peat pellets* that have been soaked in water, but ensure the pellets are not over saturated. A lot of growers don't like them, though, and an alternative is 7.5cm pots filled with a good quality 'seed' potting compost. Simply firm the seed compost around the stem.

Hydroponic gardeners can use rockwool starter cubes, floral foam or, alternatively, small pots can be filled with perlite or vermiculite. These hydroponic media can later be potted into soil for organic cultivation.

Whatever your potting medium, ensure that it is saturated before inserting the cuttings, but don't allow them to stand in water. You need to drain off excess liquid, as cuttings root more successfully in a well-drained medium and won't develop fungal infections.

Place the clones in a high-sided propagator with a clear plastic lid and put it under a fluorescent or MH lamp on 18 to 24 hours of daylight. Depending on the season, a greenhouse is perfect for starting young clones and won't require any lamps. It is important to maintain humidity for the early stages of the clone's life, as they have no roots. Mist them three to four times daily for the first few days, then daily with a 50% diluted feed. Ensure that the temperature remains near 24°C. You can remove the propagator cover after a few days, but continue misting the young clones and making sure that the rooting medium doesn't become waterlogged. Cuttings are repotted as soon as they start to develop roots: usually 10 to 14 days after they have been taken. Once a cutting has developed roots it can be treated as a young plant.

Air Layering

This interesting technique for propagating cuttings from plants produces strong clones from the mother. However, it's time consuming and can slow your harvesting down if you are cultivating on a large scale, as, for example, in a Sea Of Green setup. When you take a conventional cutting from a female, two fresh growing tips will appear from the node below the damaged area, effectively doubling your clone production. When applying the air layering technique, you don't physically separate the newly formed clone from its mother until it has started developing roots. This delays the healing and regeneration process, but is a small price to pay if you only require a small number of quality clones. Some plants will produce new growth tips beneath the site while the clone is still attached. The intent of air layering is to produce a rooted clone that is still attached to the mother plant, giving it an umbilical cord that allows water and nutrients to pass into the clone area. Any food produced from its own leaves above the root site is retained and utilized by the new offspring.

Select a vigorous growing tip from the mother plant and with a scalpel cut two horizontal lines just below the node, circling the stem roughly 1cm apart. Join these two rings with a vertical cut and peel the bark away. Cut through into the ***phloem,*** which is the layer beneath the bark that conducts food away from the leaves and into the plant. The phloem is tougher than the outer bark so it's not difficult to feel the depth with a little practice, just handle the scalpel gently. Scrape the phloem away with the scalpel blade, using a gentle scraping action. Try not to do damage to the ***xylem***, the layer beneath the phloem. The xylem is responsible for conducting nutrients from the plant to the leaves. It must be left intact to ensure that the clone is fed during its rooting time.

Next, apply a coating of rooting gel to the node site above the cut. Cover the whole area, including the cut, with damp sphagnum moss. Use plastic cling film wrap to hold the moss in place by wrapping it around the stem. Ensure that you leave the top and bottom of the moss exposed to aid watering and drainage. Within 10 to 14 days you'll see strong new roots developing. At this point, you can separate the clone from its mother. Remove the plastic cling wrap and treat the clone as a young plant.

Repotting Your Seedlings

Place cannabis seedlings into their final growing containers when they are between 10 and 15cm tall and show signs of vigorous growth. This helps them to form a healthy root ball in their new pots. Prepare your growing pots by filling them with fresh potting compost to within 3cm of the rim, leaving a hole in the centre for the plants. Place young plants in the containers, level with the compost mix, and firm more compost around the base of the stem.

Seedlings that were started in small pots must be carefully removed from their original containers. Place your hand over the top of the pot so that your hand is covering the soil and the plant is resting between your fingers. Then turn the pot upside down. Gently tap the base of the pot and the root ball will slide out and can be repotted into the new growing containers.

Feeding Young Plants

Potting composts contain sufficient fertilizer to sustain the young plants for the first four to six weeks of growth, depending on the size of pots you're using. After this time you have to feed the crop. For consistent and accurate feeding, use a soluble plant fertilizer that is either poured onto the compost as a drench, or sprayed directly onto the plant leaves as a foliar feed. Feed cannabis small amounts frequently, as overfeeding can be as harmful as underfeeding. Organic growers can find a range of feeds commercially available that are suitable for cannabis and are more precise than alternative methods of truly organic fertilizing, such as adding manures or nutrient tea's; produced by placing organic fertilizers in a stocking, and steeping in warm water.

Fertilizers are classified by the nutrient content, or ***NPK ratio***, enabling growers to select the most suitable type for their crop. Cannabis has varying nutrient requirements at different stages of growth.
The three main components, or macronutrients, of fertilizers are:

Nitrogen (N)
Potassium (K)
Phosphorous (P)

Vegetative Growth

Cannabis in its vegetative state requires high amounts of nitrogen in its feed. Nitrogen promotes vigorous growth and stem development; it also increases protein synthesis in the plant. Drying of the leaves and reddening of the stems, as well as stunted growth, are signs of N deficiencies. Fertilizer with an NPK of 30-15-15 is ideal for vegetative growth. This ratio indicates the percentage of macronutrients, with nitrogen the highest at 30%.

Flowering Stage

Cannabis that has entered the flowering stage requires higher amounts of phosphorous and lower levels of nitrogen. Phosphorous promotes blooming and flower production in cannabis. Dark blue/green leaves and small bud formations indicate P deficiencies. Fertilizers with an NPK of 15-30-30 are ideal for flowering.

While organic fertilizers are unsuitable for hydroponic gardening, hydroponic feeds are ideal for organic crops. To avoid overfeeding the plants, always dilute the nutrients by 50%.

Growth Promoters for Organic Gardens
Foxfarm Big Bloom, Bio Bizz, Botanicare Pure Blend and others can be used as complete nutrient sources for organic/hydroponic gardening.

Seaweed extract is available from most horticultural suppliers and contains growth stimulants. It is particularly suitable for organic production where it is used as both a root drench and a foliar spray.

Sulphate of potash supplies potassium, which is an essential partner to nitrogen and phosphate in maximizing crop yield, as well as strengthening resistance to disease. It is applied as a surface dressing to compost or soil.

Earth Food or Earth Juice is a mixture of activated carbon, amino acids, organic trace elements and lignite suspended in a catalyst of altered water. Available from hydroponic suppliers, it is highly recommended for increasing yields.

O.G.P. is the brand name for an 'organic growth promoter' manufactured in New Zealand and available in Europe. It contains extract of bee's wax and alfalfa with high levels of gibberellins that can promote strong cell growth during the vegetative period.

Hydrogen peroxide (H_2O_2) is normally associated with hydroponic cultivation; however, it is useful in organic gardening to keep down bacteria and fungi. You can add hydrogen peroxide solution to your water at each feed in the form of Oxy-Plus 17.5**%.** Alternatively, use a 35% solution of (H_2O_2) diluted at a ratio of 10 drops per four cups of water.

Watering Systems for Organic Crops

It is possible to grow an organic/hydroponic crop using commercially available feeds. You can also prepare your own organic teas by putting manures/guano into a nylon stocking and suspending it in warm water. Most organic growers store their water supply in garden water barrels or large plastic tanks in order to age it. Aging lowers the levels of chlorine in the water, allows it to be heated with aquarium heaters and, if necessary, lets you adjust the pH levels. Black plastic water tanks, available from household plumbing retailers, are generally the favoured storage tanks to use and come with their own lightproof lids. Larger tanks for commercial setups can be built from building blocks and waterproofed with a pond liner. It is not advisable to use water straight from the water mains, especially in winter when the temperature drops even lower in the underground supply pipes. Organic crops can easily be watered by hand using containers or hoses. Cultivators wanting to automate the process can use most hydroponic setups to water organic crops, with the exception of flood and drain or Nutrient Film Technique (NFT) systems, as they tend to saturate organic plants grown in potting compost.

Leaching the Soil

It is important to leach your potting composts at least once every two weeks with aged water, in order to flush out any build-up of salts. The salts come from the fertilizer solution and are deposited by evaporation in the warm grow areas. Pour aged water into each pot until it floods over the level of the soil, and then allow it to drain through. Discard the water that collects in the trays.

Supporting the Plants

Plants grown intensively in rotation will only produce a main cola with very few side shoots. However, plants grown for longer vegetative periods usually need supporting during their flowering phase, hopefully due to the weight of the buds. Short canes can be used to provide support for individual plants and are cost effective; however, some growers like to use cord supports, secured to the ceiling and attached to individual branches. Groups of plants can be supported by stretching 15cm nylon mesh horizontally above the crop. The plants grow up through the mesh and you raise it as they develop. This is a good way of supporting a large crop, although it can also be used very effectively on small flood and drain tables to support plants.

Outdoor crops usually develop thick stems and many growers collect these after harvest to use as canes and walking sticks. It is still advisable to give outdoor plants some form of support to protect them in high winds, especially if you have planted a late crop or have pruned the plants to produce two or more main colas. Growers use bamboo canes, cord or fencing wire stretched between posts, or they drive tree support stakes into the ground next to each young plant and secure them as they develop.

Alternatively, some growers cut flexible lengths of thin branches and push both ends into the soil to form an arch under each plant. These arches allow you to support individual branches more effectively, especially on cropped plants, and are better than individual canes or stakes. Check outdoor plants regularly, particularly after any heavy weather, to ensure that none have been uprooted or damaged. Damaged stems can be saved by splinting, taping and supporting the injury.

Canes used as a plant support

Horizontal netting plant support

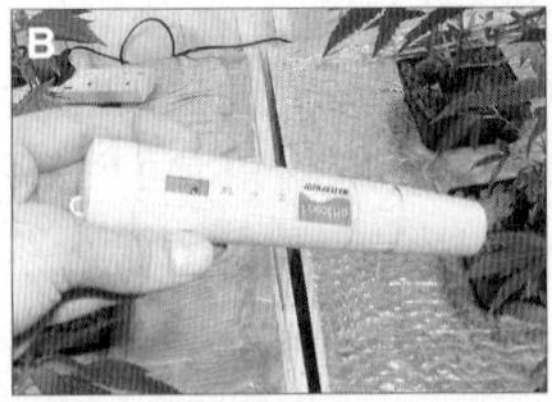

(A) Enclosed hydroponic setup using Adjust -A- Wings reflector / 1.5 kilo yield
(B) pH meter
(C) CF Truncheon used to measure dissolved solids in your reservoir

(D) Recirculating hydroponic system
(E) Ebb and flow tables

Hydro

Chapter 9

HYDROPONICS

The golden rule is that there are no golden rules. George Bernard Shaw 1856-1950

Hydroponic cultivation is growing without soil, using water that contains all of the nutrients and minerals required by a plant. In a hydroponic garden, the cultivator can control and adjust the feeding requirements to optimum levels; however, systems need careful monitoring as mistakes with the nutrient solution can ruin a crop.

Measuring pH Levels in the Nutrient Solution

pH is a measurement of acidity or alkalinity. On a scale measuring 1 to 14, neutral would be 7. The lower the reading, the more acidic the solution:

1 to 7 is called an 'acid' and 7 to 14 is an 'Alkaline' solution

The ideal pH range for cannabis cultivation is 6.5 in soil and about 5.5 in most hydroponic solutions. Be aware that extremes of pH will cause serious injury to cannabis plants. pH is measured in the solution using either a digital meter or pH test papers. You dip the test papers into the solution and compare the colour changes to the chart that is supplied. Meters are more accurate and convenient to use. Serious growers should invest in a professional pH meter unit with a detachable probe.

Adding phosphoric acid, sulphuric acid or white vinegar lowers pH in nutrient solutions. Add small amounts and check until the meter shows the required reading. Sodium hydroxide, potassium hydroxide or baking soda will raise pH levels. pH adjusters are toxic and aggressive chemicals, so always store them safely and protect your skin and eyes when using them.

Measuring the Nutrient Strength

The standard measurement of nutrient concentration in hydroponic solutions is known as Total Dissolved Solids (TDS) and is expressed in parts per million (ppm). To gauge the TDS in a solution you require a meter that measures Electrical Conductivity (EC) or Conductivity Factor (CF), which is the ability of a solution to conduct an electric current. Pure, distilled water contains no minerals and so cannot conduct electricity. As nutrients are added the conductivity will increase. Measuring this gives the cultivator an accurate method of determining nutrient strength. TDS are confusing and most growers use EC (CF) units of measure. The standard used for the measurement of EC is milli-Siemens per centimetre (mS/cm). In order for your meter to show a reading in TDS it has to convert the EC reading using a mathematical equation; however, different meter manufacturers use different factors (0.50 to 0.72) to calculate the ppm they display, although the EC/CF reading will be the same for all meters. To convert EC to CF multiply by 10.

Standard hydroponic nutrient solutions are EC 2.0 *milliSiemens* (or 2.omS/cm^2) or 20 CF units. Hydroponic solutions should be within the parameters 1.5 mS – 2.0mS

Nutrient Requirements of Cannabis Plants

Essential nutrients in hydroponic fertilizers are classified as either macronutrients that are required in large amounts or micronutrients that are required in smaller quantities. Along with essential nutrients, plants require carbon, oxygen and hydrogen, which are supplied by water and the atmosphere.

Water (H_2O)

Most hydroponic feeds come in either grow or bloom formulations, as plants have different requirements at different stages. Hydroponic feeds are also formulated for hard or soft water. Hard water has high levels of bicarbonates in the form of magnesium and calcium salts that cause a build-up of salt deposits, locking up trace minerals. It is easy to identify hard water areas by the build-up of lime scale in kettles. The main problem for the hydroponic gardener is that the bicarbonates require large amounts of acid to neutralize them before the pH can be adjusted. Growers in hard water areas need to use hard water formulations. If you only have a small number of plants, try using mineral water. Mineral water contains trace elements and carbonated waters contain CO_2 as does rainwater. Tap water is treated with chlorine and in some areas fluoride, so most growers allow the water to stand or age before using it. Excessive amounts of chlorine will cause a hardening of the crop. Run tap water before filling your reservoirs to disperse any sediment present. Hot water has high sodium and calcium deposits and should be used very sparingly, and only to warm solutions.

Hydroponic Feeds

Nutrient solutions that are designed for soil cultivation are of no use to the hydroponic grower. The feed solution must contain all of the macro and micronutrients the plant requires, and they must be in the correct balance. There are a wide variety of hydroponic solutions available that will suit indoor cannabis growers. Hydroponic nutrient packs usually come supplied in two separate containers labelled "A" and "B" for convenience. The reason behind this is that the components are incompatible with each other and cause precipitation when mixed. Once diluted into the solution there is no problem. Liquid nutrient packs are easier to use than powder formulations as the powdered feed must be dissolved before it's added to the plant reservoir. Nutrient packs recommended for hydroponic cannabis cultivation include the following:

Bush Queen Products ~ *Grow and Bloom Formulations*
Canna (Holland) ~ *Grow and Bloom Formulations*
Europonic Universal ~ *Grow and Bloom/rockwool*
General Hydroponics ~ *Flora 3 Part Feeds*
Green Haze ~ *Grow and Bloom*
Ionic ~ *Grow and Bloom Formulations*
Optimum (Growth Technology) ~ *Grow and Bloom Formulations*
Foxfarm ~ *Big Bloom,*
Bio Bizz ~ *Botanicare Pure Blend*

These packs all come with detailed instructions concerning dilution rates and are easy to use. It is important that cultivators choose a nutrient solution that is right for them and suits their hydroponic setup. Growers using rockwool may choose a solution formulated for this medium; fertilizers that are more acidic compensate for the higher pH levels caused by rockwool. However, with careful pH adjustment, all of the above nutrients can be used in rockwool setups. To optimise the uptake of the nutrient formulation you have chosen, gently heat the solution with an aquarium heater to around 24°C. The solution temperature can be monitored with a submersible thermometer purchased from an aquarium retailer.

Growth Promoters and Additives for Hydroponic Systems

Oestrogen

A diluted solution of oestrogen administered to cannabis plants can produce amazing differences in growth and flowering. Oestrogen is found in birth control pills and is diluted at the rate of 1 pill to 4 litres of water. Administer one treatment at the commencement of flowering and another treatment two weeks before harvest. Whether or not it is ethical is for you to decide.

Hydrogen Peroxide (H_2O_2)

Can be added to the solution to increase its oxygen content, thereby increasing nutrient uptake and improving photosynthesis. The addition of (H_2O_2) produces thicker plants with shorter internodal lengths and also keeps down bacteria in the solution. (H_2O_2) is sold commercially as Oxy-Plus in a 17.5% stabilized solution. Alternatively, it can be purchased from hairdressing wholesalers, who sell it as hair bleach. Add one teaspoon of 35% (H_2O_2) per 20 litres of nutrient solution, twice a week. Dip test strips into the reservoir to give a reading. The optimum level is 30 to 50 ppm.

Nitrozyme

A growth enhancer that can be added to the nutrient solution or used as a foliar feed. It contains *cytokinins*, which are hormones derived from a North Atlantic sea plant. They aid in cell division and enlargement. Use Nitrozyme in early plant development but not during flowering.

Seaweed Extract
Contains natural growth stimulators and is available commercially in Europe. It is excellent for both organic and hydroponic cultivation, and can be used as a foliar spray or root drench. The extract will mix readily with any foliar feeds you choose to use.

Adding a ***non-ionic wetting agent*** to the spray will increase uptake of foliar feeds. Wetting agents work by increasing the surface tension of water, allowing the nutrients to penetrate deep into the leaf tissue. Alternatively, add a few drops of liquid dish detergent, rinsing the plant leaves regularly with fresh water to avoid blocking the stomata. Recommended growth enhancers for hydroponic cannabis crops are:

Bcuzz Boosters ~*Promotes both growth and flowering*
Hydrosphere Energizer ~*Use during flowering*
Power Bloom ~*Females produce better flowers*
Sensa Spray ~*Hormonal stimulant*
Superthrive ~*Vitamin and hormone concentrate*
Wilder Leaf and Flower ~*Growth and flowering*

Flushing
Hydroponic cultivators can produce smoother tasting cannabis flowers by flushing the plants prior to harvesting. Flushing removes any chemical residue that may have built up in the crop, and is recommended because nitrate salts (a form of nitrogen in NPK) are not healthy to smoke. The hydroponic feed is replaced with pure pH-adjusted water for the last three days of flowering. There are commercial hydroponic flushes available that are added to the water; however, some growers prefer to reduce the strength of the nutrient solution, as opposed to flushing it through with water. A gradual reduction over the last two weeks before harvest tends to work best.

Aim to have the solution at 25% strength by the last day.

Troubleshooting Hydroponic Systems

If problems occur with your crop, first check that all plants are suffering from the same symptoms. The plants themselves are the best indicator of problems within your setup, so check your crop daily.

Symptom	Potential Problem
Black Leaf	Temperature fluctuations. Parasitic insects
Copper Leaf	Feed problems. Saturated medium. Nutrients
Droop Leaf	Feed problems. Dry Medium. Fungus gnat larvae
Irregular Leaf	Over feeding. Nutrient solution. Parasitic insects
Leaf Drop	Feed problems. Dry medium. Extreme temp
Stunted	Feed problems. Low light levels. Parasitic insects
Wilting	Check irrigation. Check for insect attack on roots
Yellow Leaf	Under feeding. Saturated medium. Low light levels

New growth problems are almost always associated with the nutrient solution – usually a deficiency of nutrients, or a build up of toxicity. Either way, the remedy is to replace the solution in the reservoir after flushing the system through with fresh water. Hydroponic crops recover quickly once the nutrient solution has been changed and adjusted. As a precautionary measure, flush the system with fresh water every eight weeks. Most problems with your hydroponic crop will be environment-based, rather than with the nutrient solution itself.

Low light levels will produce weak, thin plants with pale leaves: a condition known as *chlorosis*.

Temperature problems will cause wilting and black or brown leaves, irregular growth and weak plants.

Humidity problems will cause fungal attacks and stunted growth.

Daily Check List

1. Assess the condition of the plants. Are there any signs of insect attack? Check the condition of the new growth, and the colour and vigour of the plants.

2. Assess the condition of the growing medium: Do algae formations exist? Is the medium waterlogged? Are the visible roots white and healthy? Does the medium smell fresh?

3. Assess the environmental conditions. Are the temperature, humidity and light at the correct levels?

4. Assess whether the system is functioning correctly. Check solution for pH and EC/CF. Test pumps, fans, vents, and CO_2 equipment.

5. Assess to ensure that light is not escaping or entering the grow room.

Hydroponic Media

The most productive way to grow cannabis hydroponically involves using an inert, sterile medium to support the plant roots. The medium does not contain any nutrients or minerals of its own; they are supplied to the plant during the irrigation process, either by hand or using an automated system. Gravel, sand, foam, and even beads have all been used for hydroponic cultivation. The best media for hydroponic cannabis cultivation are:

Rockwool

Rockwool is a lightweight, sterile growing medium available in slabs, cubes or granules. Rockwool can be used in all hydroponic setups, although its pH value is quite high at around 7.5. The nutrient solution must be adjusted to compensate for this high pH value. There are specially formulated feeds designed for rockwool setups but, as long as the nutrient solution is kept more acidic, any hydroponic packs can be used. Rockwool will easily hold up to 10 times more water than soil, but like all hydroponic media it is less forgiving and provides no buffer against fluctuating pH levels. Rockwool provides an ideal environment for algae growth on its exposed surfaces and, although this growth is not harmful to the plants and doesn't compete for food, it can encourage fungus gnats and caspid flies, so cover all exposed surfaces with aluminium foil or lightproof polythene. Dry rockwool is an irritant so wear gloves when handling it.

Greenmix and Golden Wool

Greenmix and Golden Wool are tufts of rockwool granulate that have a mixture of water absorbent and repellent properties that makes them particularly good for hydroponic cultivation.

Perlite

Perlite is an inert granular growing medium that is produced at very high temperatures and used in containers to provide a lightweight, sterile, absorbent material in which to cultivate. Saturated perlite will hold just as much air as rockwool and can be reused but needs careful cleaning to remove any dead roots and must be sterilized. It is advisable to cover the tops of the pots with foil to prevent algae from forming. Perlite can be reused but ensure it is cleaned and sterilized.

Coconut Fibre

Coconut fibre holds more water and oxygen than rockwool, which is an advantage in passive hydroponic systems. Unlike most hydroponic media, coconut fibre is completely natural: it contains organic compounds and is environmentally friendly. Dutch cultivators have been using 50% coconut fibre mixed with 50% expanded clay pebbles with excellent results. Choose a coarse coconut fibre prepared for hydroponic cultivation. Coconut fibres intended for adding to potting composts can be too finely graded and high in sodium.

Clay Pebbles

Clay pebbles are porous, lightweight and pH-neutral and can be used in active hydroponic setups, but are not good at lifting nutrients from reservoirs in passive systems. Used alone in ebb and flow systems, clay pebbles are too light and can result in the plants falling over during the flood cycle. As clay pebbles can be reused indefinitely, they are cost effective and make a useful medium to mix with coconut fibre. Clay pebbles are usually imported and sold in metric sizes. The most popular sizes are 8 to 16mm. Choose a brand that looks irregular in shape with no smooth round pebbles as the small crevices and pockets help feeder roots form.

Vermiculite

Vermiculite is a very absorbent, lightweight growing medium that holds water well. Because it is excellent at drawing nutrients in passive hydroponic systems such as wick units, vermiculite is used as the bottom layer under perlite. Vermiculite can become waterlogged when used on its own, but is ideal for germinating seeds.

Hydroponic Systems

Hydroponic setups are classified as either active or passive. Active systems use pumps to distribute the nutrients to the plants and passives do not. Those suitable for compost watering systems are marked: ☑

Aeroponics

Aeroponics is a hydroponic method of propagating and growing plants in air. Plants are grown with their roots suspended in a lightproof, sterile and enclosed air chamber where a nutrient vapour is pulse-sprayed onto the developing roots – in some systems more than 200 times every 12 hours. Aeroponic propagation is not new, it was first used in 1944, but advances in modern technology have allowed us to build more efficient aeroponic systems. Most growers prefer to buy ready-made aeroponic setups, but it is possible to build a unit yourself providing you understand the principles. An aeroponics chamber can be constructed from a black plastic, domestic plumbing tank. The clone is put in a net pot or perforated container holding an inert growing medium, such as rockwool or clay pebbles. The container sits in a small opening cut into the removable lid and is supported to allow the roots to hang in the lightproof chamber. A drain placed at the bottom of the tank allows you to collect the nutrient mix in a reservoir and reuse it by placing a pump in the reservoir to force water up a pipe to feed a misting nozzle that is fixed into the growth chamber. It is best to connect the pump to a digital timer programmed to spray at 15-minute intervals.

You can build a unit like this using a powerful submersible pump, connected by a hose to misting nozzles taken from hand-held garden sprayers, and it will work well. Use a commercially available hydroponic feed at the manufacturer's recommended dilutions (pH 5.5) and add either seaweed extract or one of the many growth-promoting supplements that are commercially available. Aeroponics is not the best system for novices but with a little experience it can produce very high-yielding crops.

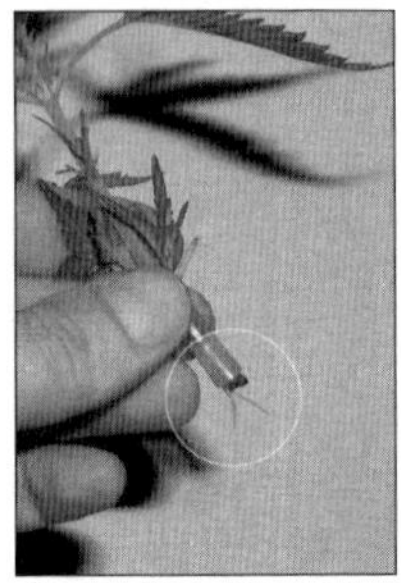

Aeroponics: clone after 7 days in an aero-cloner

Aeroponic Chamber

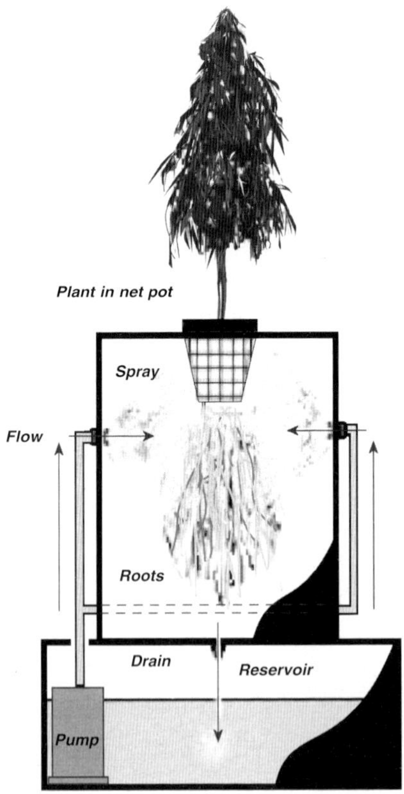

Aeroponic Cloning

An aero-cloner is simple to make using a lightproof, plastic container with a tightfitting lid. The size of your container is governed by the number of clones you want to produce. If you only require a small number then kitchen storage containers are ideal. Lightproof your container by painting the outside with black rubber paint. Next, the container base is fitted with an aquarium bubble bar that can be bought inexpensively at an aquarium supplier. The bar requires an air pump, available at the same supplier, and is connected using flexible tubing. Choose one that produces a fine stream of bubbles and secure it to the base of your container using silicon glue. The bubble bar should cover most of the container length so larger setups will require additional bars. The container is now partly filled with pure pH-adjusted water and the air pump is switched on. The bubble bar creates tiny splashes at the water's surface that spray the clone stems. You will need to adjust the water depth to ensure the spray hits the stems but does not submerge them. The clones are supported in a series of 10mm holes drilled into the container lid that enables the plant stems to hang just above the water. The clones are first placed in 3cm lengths of 10mm plastic tubing. Split the tubing down one side so you can easily remove the rooted clones. These tube supports should fit neatly into the holes in the lid. You can test the aero-cloner by closing the lid and running the air pump. If it is running correctly you should see splashes of water coming up through the empty holes in the lid. Once you have your cuttings in position and the air pump running continuously, they should root in about 7 to 10 days. There is no requirement to feed the clones.

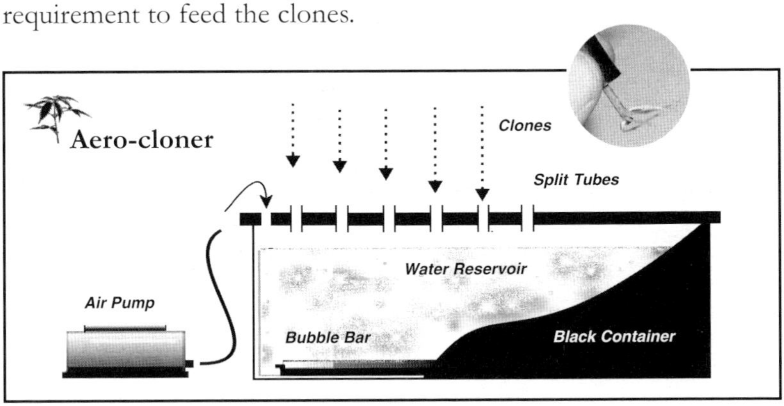

Deep Water Culture (DWC)

The basic requirements for healthy root growth are water, nutrients and oxygen. Providing cannabis roots receive a plentiful supply of oxygen, they can be kept permanently submerged in a light (one third strength) nutrient solution. This allows growers to set up a very simple, hydroponic bubbler system that can produce surprisingly heavy yields. Ensure that your container holds a minimum of 15 litres. A plastic bucket with a tight -fitting lid is ideal but should be light-proofed to prevent unwanted algae growth within the chamber. Oxygen is supplied to the nutrient solution by an aquarium bubble bar or airstone that is connected to an air pump with flexible tubing. The bubble bar is placed in the container through a small hole in the lid. If you are using an airstone, ensure that it is weighted down so that it sits on the bottom of the bucket.

The container only holds one plant that is placed in a 15cm net pot containing your chosen medium and fits tightly into a hole cut into the plastic lid. You can grow more than one plant in a DWC solution; you just need a larger reservoir to create a bath. Ensure that the nutrient solution is kept between 2 and 2.5cm above the bottom of the net pot. This is best measured using a gauge made by pushing a thin plastic drinking straw into a small square of polystyrene. Next, cut a 4cm section from a larger diameter straw and glue this into position in a small hole cut into the container lid. The polystyrene floats on the nutrient surface and the nutrient level is shown by the thin straw that slides up and down the larger section glued to the lid. You can easily calibrate the high and low measure by marking the sliding straw.

Leave the airstone running continually and keep the solution's pH constant at around 5.5. Ensure that your nutrient solution remains at one-third strength throughout the plant's growth cycle. This can be easily calculated using the manufacturer's recommendations.

DWC Bubbler Unit

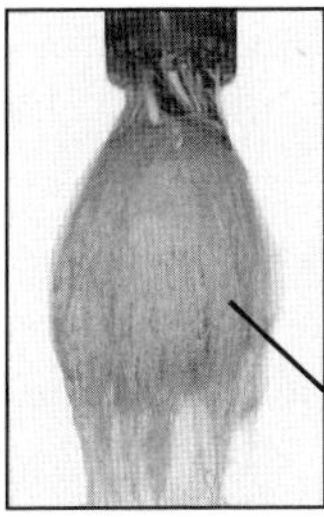

Roots grow down into the nutrient reservoir

Remember to keep the nutrient solution at 1/3 strength. Do not use a full strength solution at any time!

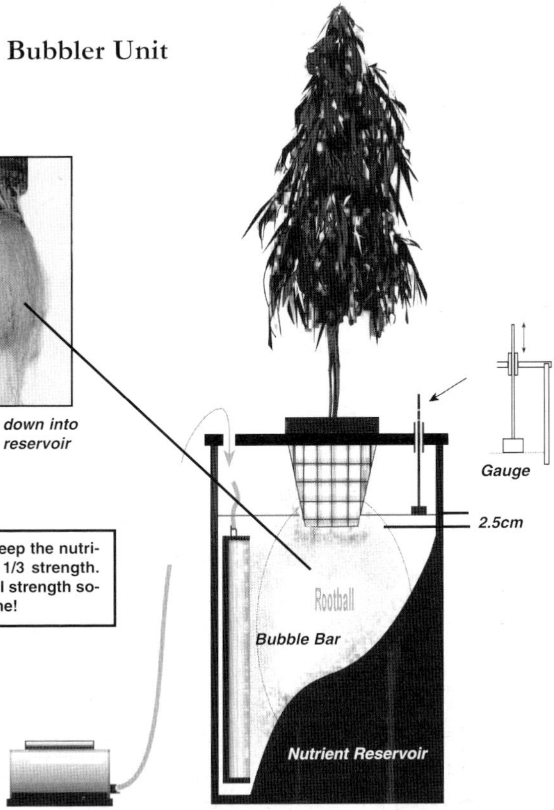

Hydroponic retailers can supply you with ready-made DWC kits

Good bud development on DWC plant

Pot Culture ☑

Pot culture is the simplest form of hydroponic cultivation and involves growing each plant in its own container, filled with any of the popular hydroponic media. Most growers prefer perlite, coconut fibre or rockwool granulate. Despite its simplicity, excellent results can be achieved using this system. It is, however, difficult to automate. Choose a pot with a 10 to 15-litre capacity and place it into a deep saucer or tray to act as a reservoir.

Always water from the top, allowing the reservoir to fill up. Small plants will require watering every two to three days but mature plants will require daily feeding. Allow the reservoir to almost empty before feeding again as this draws air down into the medium. Leach the medium every two to three weeks to prevent a buildup of salts.

Large mothers used for rotation setup grown in plastic buckets / pot culture

Wick Systems ☑

Wick systems are a simple but effective method of growing hydroponic crops. Nylon cord is threaded through the drainage holes in the bottom of the pot so that it passes up one hole, across, and down out of the opposite hole. This is repeated so that you have two lengths of cord threaded through, leaving four ends hanging down. Trim the lengths so that they are about 15cm long. Next, add a layer of vermiculite to a depth of 3cm and fill the remaining space with perlite or coconut fibre. Then suspend the pot over the nutrient reservoir and water it from the top to saturate the medium. As the plant feeds, it will draw nutrients up the wick by capillary action.

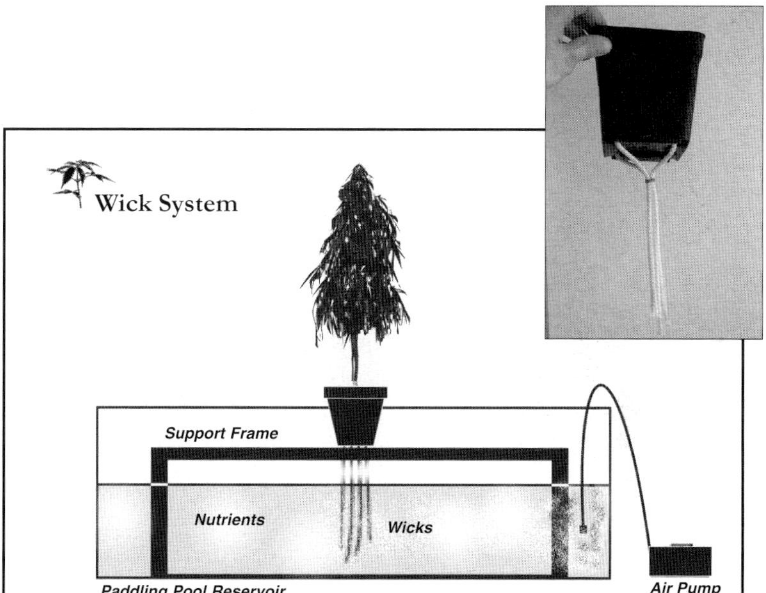

Wick systems have their limitations but can be useful in some setups. Organic growers can use wicks to draw nutrient free water to the crop but as with hydroponic wick systems, ensure that your reservoir is light proofed and covered

Capillary Floor System (CFS) ☑

Thick polythene sheeting is laid onto a level grow room floor in strips between one and two metres across (depending on your lamps wattage). A framework of 5 x 5cm timber is laid around the polythene edge that is then stapled to it, producing a large waterproof tray. Capillary matting is then laid right up to the 5cm lip. Ensure that any joins are overlapped by at least 5cm. The matting is now saturated with nutrient solution and covered with lightproof, reflective plastic sheeting. Individual plants are prepared by placing them into 15cm pots of perlite, coconut fibre or wrapped rockwool cubes. A cross is cut into the polythene cover, taking care not to cut into the matting or base plastic, and the edges lifted so that the pot or cube sits on the mat. The plant roots will grow out into the matting, but the plants will need supporting, as they cannot form a vertical root system. The root growth is not affected by this: the roots just spread horizontally across the mat. Stretch a horizontal section of wide mesh nylon netting between the posts to act as support.

The system is easily automated using a sump pump and timer but ensure that your feed hose runs up one metre vertically before branching off: this prevents siphoning once the pump has stopped. You need to calculate how long the feeding takes and set your timer accordingly. The matting needs to be saturated but not swamped. These setups need feeding with nutrient-free water, once every 7th feed. Collect a sample of this from the matt area and test its pH and EC. Your next feed can then be adjusted to compensate for any fluctuations.

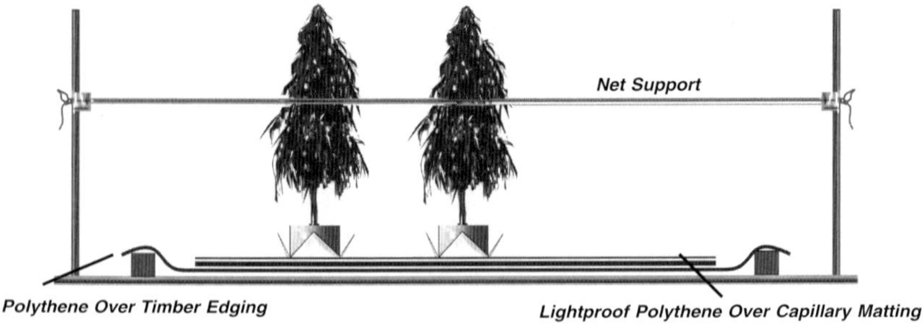

Gravity Fed Systems ☑

Nutrient solution can be placed into a lightproof reservoir that is then suspended and lowered manually, to water the plants. The reservoir needs a small breather hole in the top to allow the solution to flow properly. A section of hose is connected to the base of the table to allow the solution to run in and out of the flood area, where it acts in the same way as a flood and drain table. By lowering the reservoir beneath the flood area after each watering, the unused solution can be drawn back into the reservoir through the delivery tube (see *p73*). Grow tables require flooding at least twice a day, which can cause problems for some cultivators, but an alternative drip system can be built and left for several days with proper management.

It is possible to incorporate a drip system that works by gravity feed, but it requires a large reservoir to ensure you have sufficient water pressure to deliver the nutrients evenly to each plant. The reservoir for a gravity drip system is permanently positioned above the height of the grow table. The solution run-off is collected in a container positioned under a drain hole at the base of the grow table and manually poured back into the reservoir.

These systems are easy to design and build yourself. They allow the grower a degree of automation and do not require any power to work pumps. They are particularly well suited for greenhouses and outdoor hydroponics in remote areas.

Gravity setups can be used to water organic crops but you must take care not to saturate the growing medium. Allow the potting compost to dry out slightly before you water, this will prevent the medium becoming waterlogged and allow the roots to breathe. It is not advisable to use automated flood and drain tables for organic cultivation but the gravity setup at least ensures that you only flood when the plants require it.

For this reason gravity systems are marked ☑

Flood and Drain

Also known as "Ebb and Flow" these setups are very effective and consistently produce high-yielding crops. Plants are grown on a waterproof tray table with 15cm sides. The table stands over a reservoir filled with nutrients and is connected by a 1.5cm hose that is attached to a submersible fountain or sump pump. The plants stand on the table in pots filled with perlite, Golden Wool, clay pebbles, or coconut fibre, or you can use wrapped rockwool cubes. Some growers fill the table itself with clay pebbles and plant directly into it.

At least twice during the day cycle a programmable timer switches on the submersible pump. The pump forces nutrients up the hose and into the growing tray. The plants are watered from the base up with the liquid forcing stale air out of the pots as it rises. When the pump stops, the nutrients drain back down the hose under the force of gravity and into the reservoir. This action draws fresh air into the pots as the solution drains out of the medium and ensures that the plant roots are well aerated. An overflow is fitted to ensure that the tray doesn't overfill. It is important for the table to be level so that all the plants receive the same amount of nutrients. The nutrients should be checked regularly and adjusted.

An aquarium heater will keep the solution at 24°C and although some growers like to add a fish tank air pump to keep the feed fresh and aerated, this is not necessary as the solution is regularly moving.

These systems are easy for the grower to build using plywood, waterproofed with glass fibre or polythene. The reservoir is made from plastic water storage tanks available at plumbing supply outlets. Alternatively, these flood and drain systems can be purchased ready-made from hydroponic suppliers. It is advisable to cover the tops of the trays with reflective, lightproof polythene, secured along the edges. Cut into the cover to place your plants on the tray. This prevents evaporation, inhibits the formation of algae, and the reflective surface bounces light back to the underside of the plants.

Flood and Drain

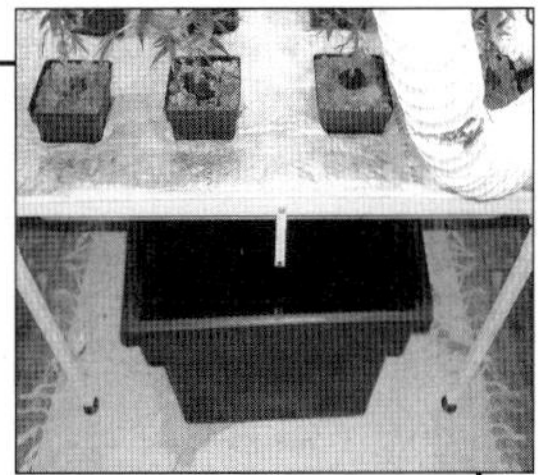

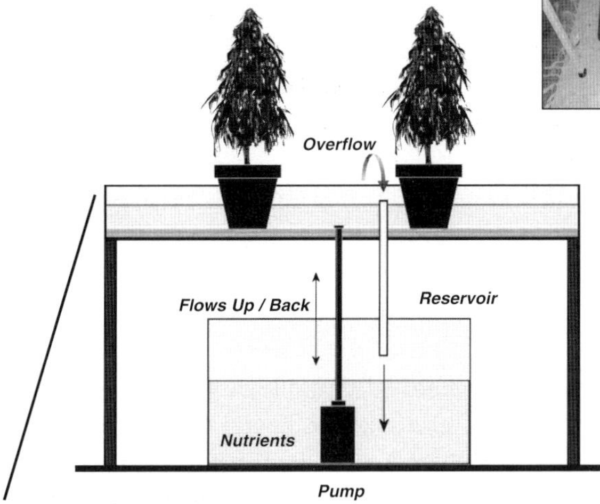

Roots develop under the cover

Gravity Fed

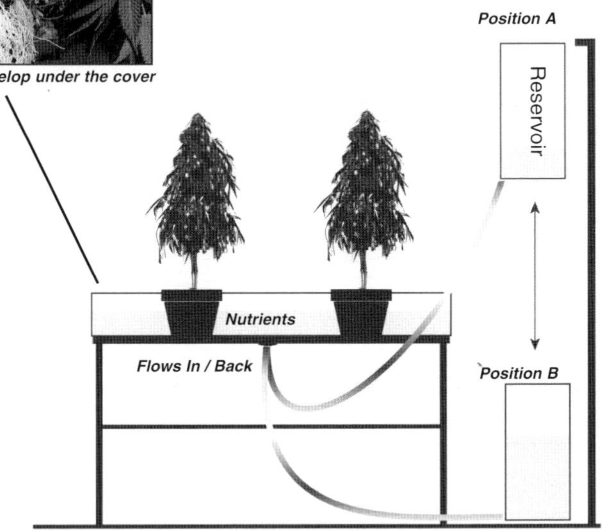

Nutrient Film Technique (NFT)

This method of hydroponic cultivation involves continuously recirculating nutrients around the plant roots. The plants are grown on a gently sloping tray that runs into the reservoir. A pump in the reservoir forces nutrients up to the top of the tray, where they run back down under the force of gravity. Capillary matting ensures that the nutrients are evenly distributed to the plants.

The plants can be in wrapped rockwool cubes or 15cm pots of perlite, Golden Wool or coconut fibre. Cover the capillary matting with lightproof polythene and cut out sections for the plant pots or cubes to sit in.

The reservoir has a removable lid that allows you to test and adjust the solution as required. An aquarium heater keeps the solution at 24°C and the nutrients are well aerated by the constant movement so you don't need an air pump. You can easily build this system or one can be bought ready-made from your hydroponics supplier.

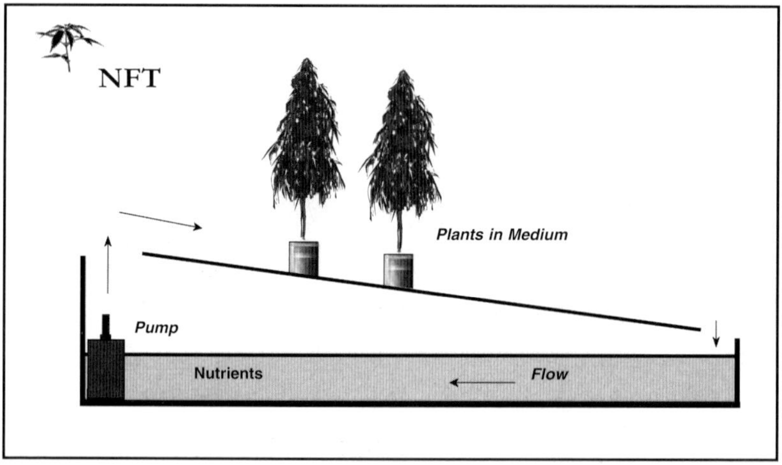

Rockwool Culture Slabs

Rockwool culture slabs are widely used in European commercial horticulture and are a convenient way of growing cannabis plants. The 15cm and 20cm slabs are best suited to cannabis cultivation. Grodan produce plastic trays that the slabs fit into and they make an excellent passive system that can be watered by hand in smaller setups. The plants are brought on in wrapped rockwool cubes that are placed into cuts made in the plastic cover on the slab to allow the roots to grow down through it.

Placing the slabs into open-ended sloping channels makes an excellent recirculating, active system. Position the channel above a reservoir so that the nutrients can be collected and reused. Generally, crops are cultivated in rows of these channels that are positioned on a raised timber support. The nutrient run-off is collected in a section of plastic roof gutter that is placed across the bottom of the channels and directs the solution back into the reservoir where it can be recirculated. The nutrient solution is delivered to the base of each individual plant with a constant drip system.

Rockwool Culture Slabs

Rockwool Cube

Clones can be rooted in small rockwool starter cubes before being placed into the larger cubes positioned on the rockwool culture slab

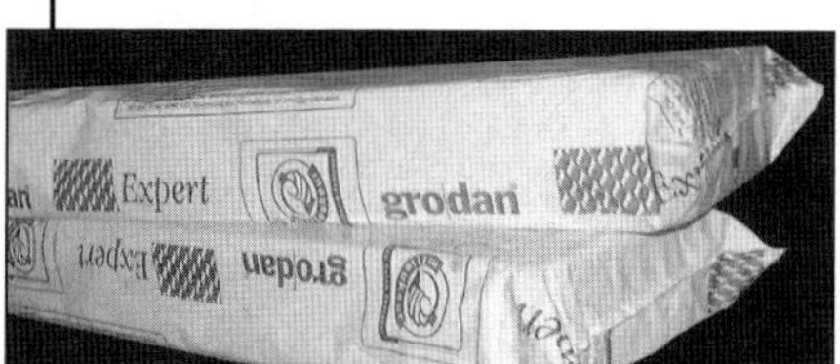

Rockwool Slabs

Drip Irrigation ☑

These setups use small bore spaghetti tubing that branch off a larger feed hose to deliver a constant flow of nutrients to the base of each individual plant in the system. The flow is regulated by the use of special drip emitters that fit on the end of the tubing and are available from horticultural suppliers, along with the spaghetti tubing. The tubing is supported on a small plastic stake that is placed into the medium to ensure the dripping solution is directed to the base of the plant. As an alternative to fitting expensive drip control valves, you can simply bend the last 3cm of pipe back against itself and hold it securely in place using garden wire. This can then be adjusted to regulate the flow. Drip systems can be either *closed*, where the nutrient is collected from the run-off trough and recirculated, or *open* where the feed is allowed to run to waste. Open systems are not recommended for cultivators, as they are a waste of resources. Providing your nutrient solution is regularly monitored and adjusted, it can be recirculated for weeks. Perlite, Golden Wool, coconut fibre or rockwool cubes are all good growing media to use in drip systems. The setup can also be used to water organic crops, and is especially useful in greenhouse cultivation where you may have large numbers of plants to irrigate. The drippers can be set to deliver the plants exact water requirements. Any feeding you need to carry out is simply added to the reservoir ensuring that each plant receives the correct amount of nutrients. The fertilizers are delivered slowly over a longer period than conventional watering, which is a more efficient way of delivering nutrient solutions to the plants.

These systems can be built using corrugated plastic roofing sheets and standing each plant container or cube on them. The sheets are held in position with a simple timber frame and angled downwards to allow the solution to drain off. A section of roof gutter or eaves troughing is attached across the bottom of the run to collect the used nutrients and can either lead to the reservoir or to a drain. Submersible pumps are used to move the nutrients through the system and, due to its constant flowing action; the solution does not need aerating.

Drip Irrigation Table

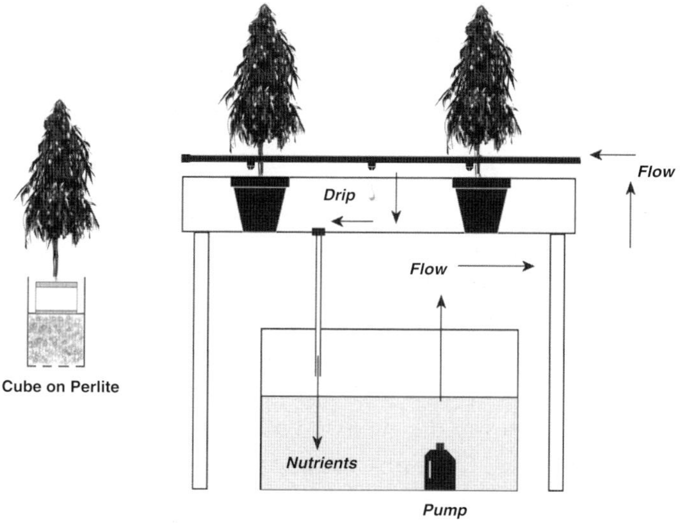

Drip emitters branch from the main supply pipe to feed every plant in this setup

The Plastic Channel Technique

This setup is built onto a gently sloping surface made from plywood. The system needs to stand roughly 90cm off the floor at the high end and less at the low end so that a child's paddling pool can fit underneath and act as the reservoir. Alternatively, you can build the system higher and use a water tank. The reservoir needs to be wider in order to catch the run-off. Or, fix a section of guttering across and underneath, to direct the flow back into the reservoir. A 40cm wide strip of thick, lightproof polythene is laid from the top of the plywood run to the bottom, dead centre, and allowed to overhang slightly.

The very top of the strip is tacked in place before a 10cm strip of capillary matting is run centrally down the whole length. Cannabis plants in 10cm rockwool cubes are placed down the strip, leaving 30cm between the stems. Once you have filled the strip, the two edges are folded up and over the cube in a triangular shape and secured with staples, bulldog clips or clothes pegs.

All that you should see are the plants growing from the spaces left in the triangular channel. This procedure is repeated, leaving 30cm between centres, until the board is full. A hose is run up from the tank and branched so that each run is fed. A submersible pump is fitted to the hose and then nutrients are pumped up to the top of each channel and allowed to run down under the force of gravity. Ensure that you have left enough of an overhang at the base of the channel to direct the nutrient back into the reservoir. Cover the remainder of the reservoir with polythene to act as a lid. Heat the solution to 24°C and leave it feeding continuously.

The plastic channel technique is used in larger setups and is a cost-effective way of building a system that can be used both indoors and out. The system helps to keep humidity levels manageable in grow rooms, as the heat of the lamps does not easily evaporate the nutrient.

Plastic Channel Technique

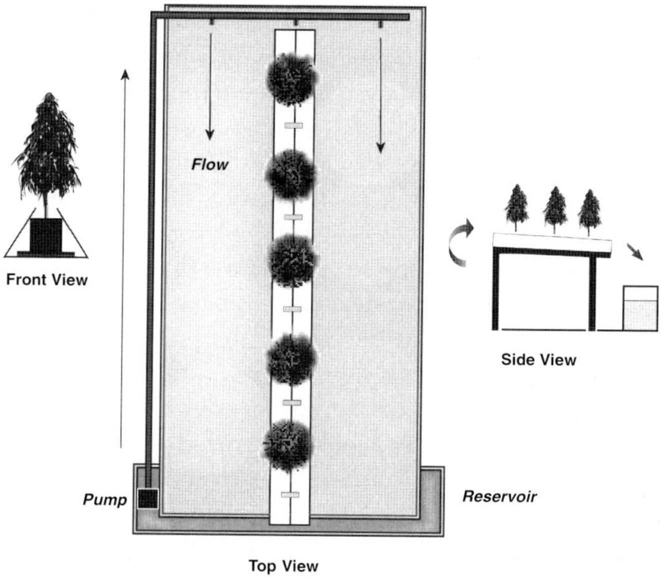

Approximate Light For Your Table

As with all indoor grows your plastic channel table requires a *<u>minimum</u>* *50-watts of HID lighting per 30cm² of illuminated area:*

1x70-watt HID = 30cm x 30cm garden
1x 250-watt HID = 60cm x 60cm garden
1x 400-watt HID = 85cm x 85cm garden
1x 600-watt HID = 105cm x 105cm garden
1x 1000-watt HID = 120cm x 120cm garden

Remember: 3 x 600-watt HID's will give better light distribution than 2 x 1000-watt in the same grow area, despite having less intensity!

Tube Systems

Plastic drainage pipes can be used to build effective active hydroponic systems. 15cm tubes are cut to the desired length, usually two metres, and placed on a wooden frame constructed to support them. The frame slopes gently and has semicircular cuts to accommodate the base of the tubing. It is usual to have four pipes sitting next to each other in the frame, but larger setups can be built. The ends of the four pipes are sealed with rubber caps that are available from the building supplier where you purchase the plastic tubing.

The pipes need a series of circular holes, 20 to 30cm apart, cut in a straight line along the top. Use an electric drill fitted with a special cutting bit and make the holes large enough for a 10cm net pot to sit in them, supported by its top lip. A reservoir is fitted underneath the frame and each pipe is connected to a 1.5cm feeder hose that is placed in a purpose-made hole at the top of the pipe's highest end. The feeder hose is branched off a submersible fountain pump and a drain is connected to the bottom of the pipe that flows back to the reservoir. The pots are filled with clay pebbles and the plants inserted. The top of the pot is covered with foil to light-seal it and the system is started. The plant roots are fed continuously with a rapidly moving oxygenated nutrient solution and will grow down into the tubing. Excellent results are possible with this system.

As an alternative, you can build a PVC pipe system from inverted plastic drink bottles, painted white with the bases cut off so they can be fixed into couplers on 5cm plastic, plumbing waste pipes. A ball rolled from durable netting material is placed in each base to act as a particle filter and the plants are then placed into the inverted bottles in rockwool cubes or an inert medium. A drip system is used to feed each plant and the run-off is collected via the connected pipes and held in a reservoir for recirculation. This system is particularly good at keeping down humidity in your grow room, and the waste pipe and couplings can be purchased cheaply from do-it-yourself stores.

Pipe System

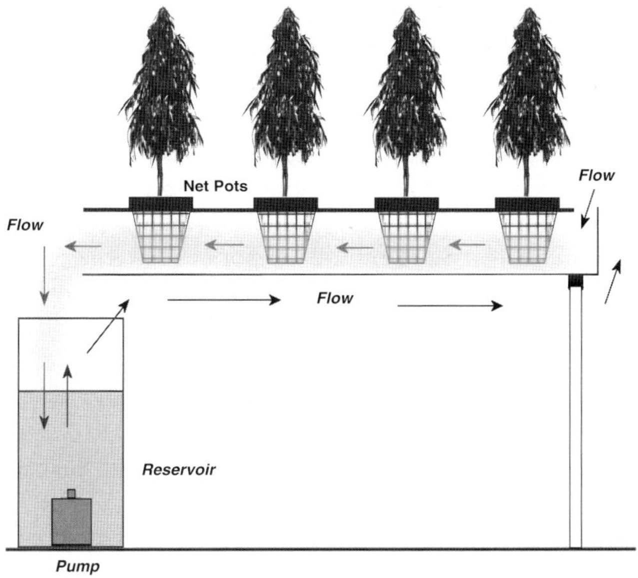

Bottle System

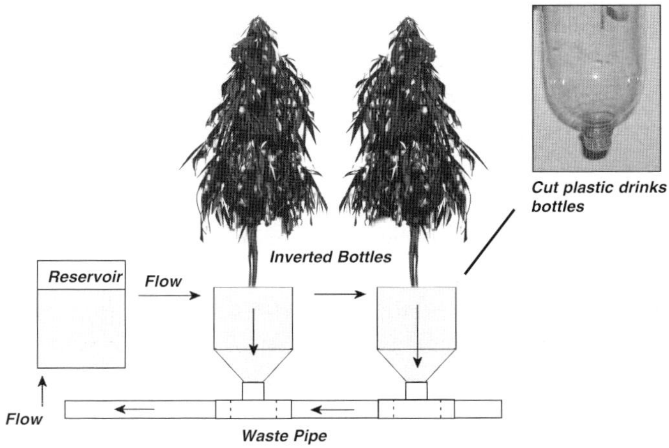

Multi-Level Systems ☑

You can maximize space within your grow area by growing the crop on shelves set at different levels. This system works particularly well for closet setups using fluorescents, but these lights have a high heat-to-light ratio and cabinet systems need careful monitoring to ensure that overheating problems don't occur. Plants are kept short and bushy by regular pruning, and CO_2 is supplied either by vents, fermentation or from gas bottles. It is easier to grow organic compost crops in shelf systems as they don't require any additional reservoirs underneath them as with hydroponic crops. Organic crops can be watered by hand and will only be the depth of the pot you have decided to use. The plant can also be repotted into larger pots as it develops and this allows the grower to use the space in the cabinet more efficiently.

Perforate the shelves in cabinet setups with a series of holes made with a 10mm drill bit. If the system is open and not using CO_2 position the exit vent in the closet roof and the intake vent in the base. This ensures that fresh air is drawn up through the setup. A small desk fan can be added to facilitate the air movement. Closed systems do not require venting, and this is one of the most effective ways of using bottled CO_2. The surfaces of the closet are lined with a reflective material to ensure good light distribution, especially when using fluorescents. An alternative to using a closet or enclosed space is to build a freestanding set of shelves and then enclose them in light reflective sheeting. To create access at the front, have a flap that can be rolled up and secure it with Velcro. Shelf systems can be built onto a wall, where space is at a premium.

The common method is to make a three-shelf arrangement that allows you to cultivate in a mini Sea Of Green (SOG) setup. One shelf is used for clones and mini-mothers, the next shelf is used for the two-week vegetative stage and the third is used for flowering. The shelves should be lightproof and enclosed so you basically end up with a closet arrangement, but you can use lightproof polythene instead of wood. Velcro the edges down and ensure a tight seal that can easily be opened and resealed.

Multi-Level Cupboard Setup

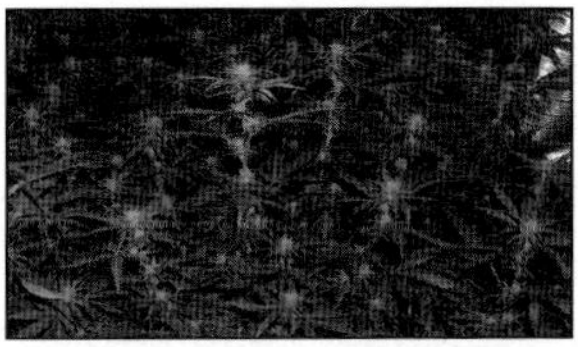

Skunk#1 budding in cupboard grow

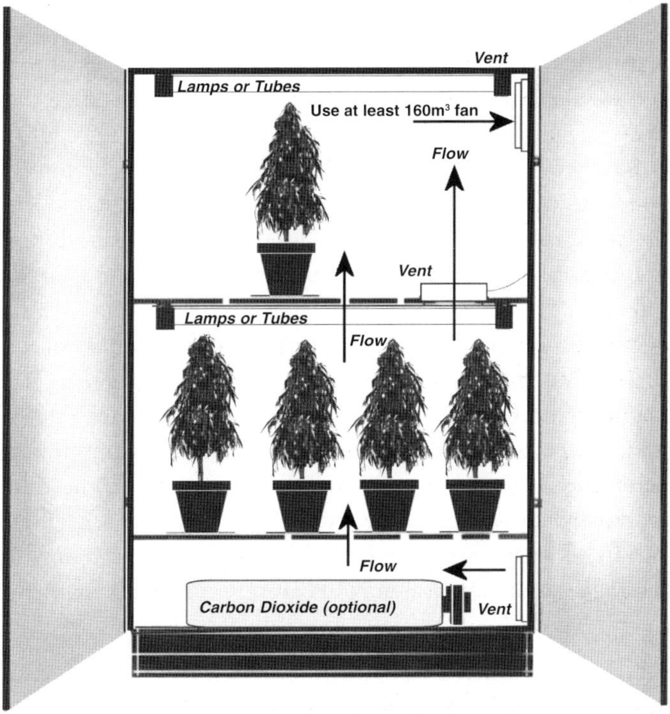

Lower shelf section of a cupboard setup. This cupboard has been split into a flowering and a vegetative section. By rotating the crops this grow yields around 50 grams per plant, every 8 weeks under 400-watt HID's. Whilst these are flowering the fresh clones are growing on above, ready to replace them

Micro systems ☑

Micro systems are run with lamps that are 100-watts or lower. These systems are ideal for the hobby grower and if you maintain your light levels at over 50-watts per 30cm square you can expect yields of more than 25-grams per square 30cm. Small HPS lamps are ideally suited for use in micro and mini systems as they provide the highest output per Watt of electricity consumed. Fluorescents and MH are not as efficient and heat buildup can be a problem when using them. To optimise yields in these small setups you need to have your plants cropped (see *Pruning*) and well inside the productive range of your lamp (this is a sphere of around 50cm for a 250-watt HPS, dropping to around 25cm for a 100-watt HPS). It is light intensity that we are interested in, and strangely, two lights with the same total wattage, as a single lamp will actually supply less intensity. This is worth noting if you intend stripping down HPS security lights for use in your system.

Micro systems are generally used to grow small numbers of pruned clones in an enclosed space. A micro system designed to house a single female can be built by constructing a plywood cabinet with a 30cm square grow area that is lined with Mylar or aluminium foil. The actual height of the grow area needs to include the depth of your pot or rockwool cube, depending on your chosen cultivation method. In addition, you include the depth of your lamp in what will become the light housing area. This area is custom built to fit your lamp.

Min box height = 30cm + height of pot/cube + light housing

The unit is lit by a small 70-watt HPS that is adapted from a garden security light. In order to prevent heat buildup in the cabinet grow area, the light is fitted above a sheet of glass that rests on battens secured inside the box. The area above the glass is enclosed and fitted with an extractor fan that is light proofed by attaching a section of ducting that is bent twice through 90°. This prevents light contamination. Fans can be adapted from bathroom extractors, computer fans or even old car parts that are run on transformers.

Some micro growers link the lamp heat extractor to a vent in the grow area itself, but if you are using CO_2 supplementation this has to be carefully controlled or you lose the gas.

Micro systems are better left as closed systems that can be given additional CO_2 through either fermentation in the grow area or gas cylinders that feed the area through a small pipe. The cylinder will last for several months since you only need to release small amounts of CO_2 gas into the growing chamber. If you are growing hydroponically then you should install a passive wick system that is fed by a small reservoir underneath the grow cabinet. Small holes are drilled into the floor of the cabinet to allow the wicks to pass down into the nutrient solution. It is possible to build an active system into a micro grow cabinet, but you are better off using a drip setup as flood systems will raise the grow area humidity to unacceptable levels. The plants are usually only given a two week vegetative cycle before flowering to ensure there is little side shoot development. If you want to give the plant a longer vegetative period then you will need to prune it in order to keep it short and bushy.

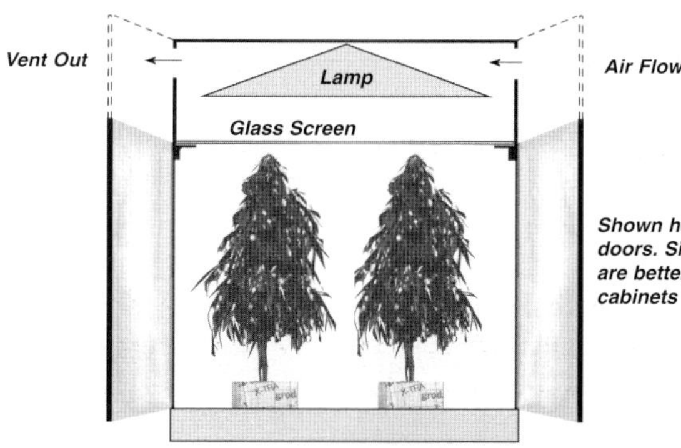

Shown here with two doors. Single doors are better for smaller cabinets up to 1m

Cabinet grow

Glass screen is clearly shown as the door is opened on this cabinet. Here the grower has a 10cm hole cut in the centre of the glass to draw air up through the grow. The intake vent is actually in the grow area itself. Window glass is ideal and can be cut to size by the retailer, ask them to cut the hole. This 1m cabinet is lit by a converted 400-watt lowbay and maintains a constant grow temperature using 1x RVK 125A1-125mm/225m³/hr fan

Mini Systems ☑

Systems are referred to as *mini* when they utilize lamps between 100 and 270-watts. A mini system can be constructed in exactly the same fashion as a micro grow cabinet. The same principles apply, only you install a stronger lamp. The grow area is made larger to take advantage of the extra lumens available. A 60cm square growing area can hold two female clones using a 250-watt HPS housed above a glass screen. In mini setups you plant at a density of 1 plant per $30cm^2$.

The alternative to the grow cabinet setup is to use the Screen of Green (SCROG) method. Larger SCROG setups are covered in the next chapter and the same principles apply to mini SCROGs. A screen of chicken wire is stretched between the lamp and the flower tops, which are grown up to it, and then bent through 90° and trained horizontally underneath it. You plant at the same density but you can expect to yield around 50-grams plus per plant as the buds are grown in optimum light conditions under the wire.

SCROG

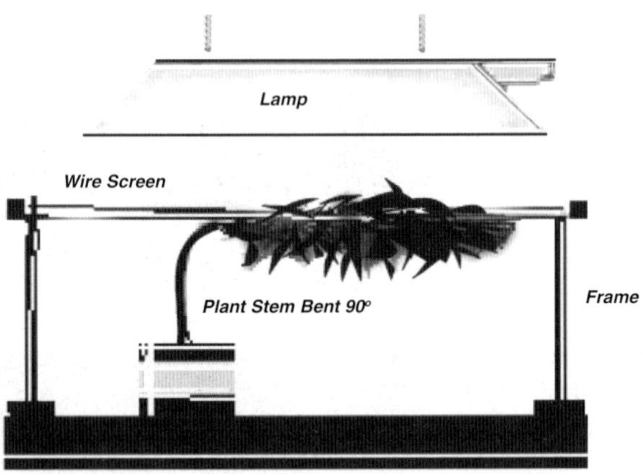

Aerospring Tank

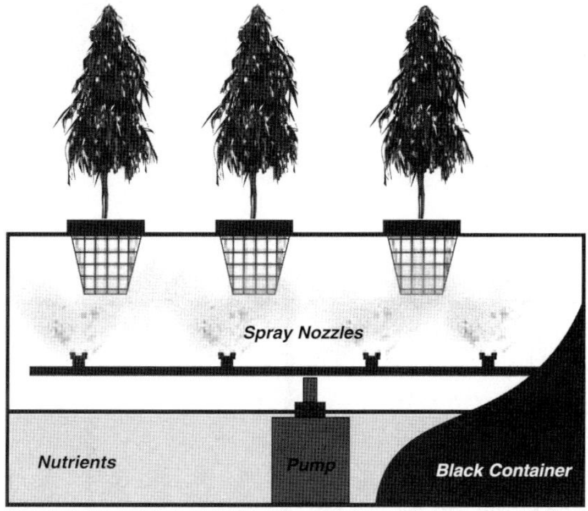

Capillary Watering Setup

Enclosed grow unit (1)

Use at least 2 x 225m³ fans and add extra inline fans to boost airflow if you have to duct any distance. Longest edge of lamp should face narrowest edge of grow for best coverage. Aim for at least 50-watts of HID per 30cm x 30cm grow area

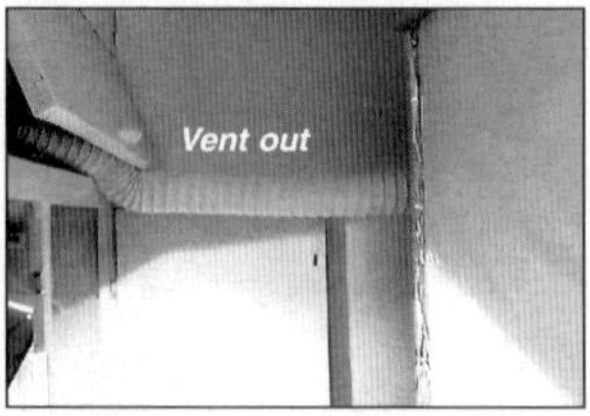

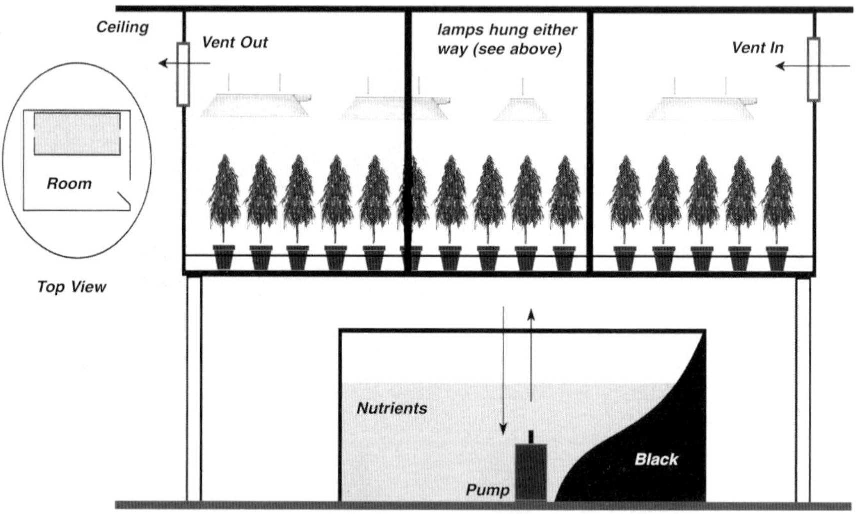

Rockwool cubes on clay pebbles

Reservoir

Enclosed grow unit (2)

Hydroponic drip system

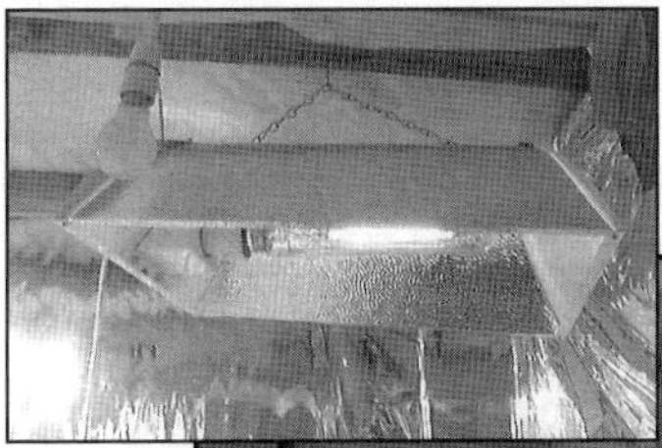

By enclosing the grow in this way you ensure no lumens are wasted from the lamps and keep odours down. Venting your grow space is easier, this setup maintains a constant grow temperature using 2 x 420m³/hr inline fans

Cuttings are placed into rockwool cubes. In this setup they are given 4 to 6 weeks vegetative growth before flowering. Longer vegetative periods produce stronger plants that will yield more

Bud formation

Dutch Sea Of Green

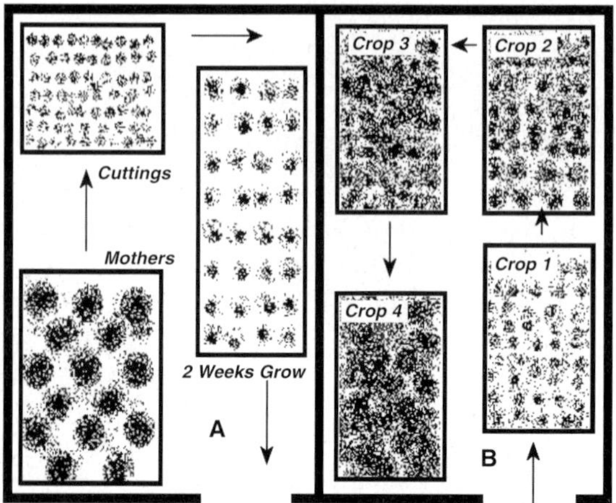

Room A / 18 Hours on 6 hours off   Room B / 12 Hours on 12 hours off

Room B

Chapter 10

GROW TECHNIQUES

It is quite a three-pipe problem. Sherlock Holmes

Dutch Sea Of Green ☑

Sea of Green (SOG) is one of the most effective techniques for producing regular cannabis crops. Using this method, it is possible to harvest a crop of sinsemilla cannabis every two weeks. There is a reduction in yield from each individual plant, but the numbers grown more than compensate.

This technique involves rotating your crop, staggering each new cloning session by two weeks. The flowering section is divided into four grow areas and is fed in two-week rotations with fresh clones. This allows you to crop every two weeks indefinitely. The SOG method is used by a lot of commercial growers, but is equally well suited to smaller setups. Shelf systems using SOG are very effective in supplying the hobby grower with a regular yield of flowers. Separate shelves are used for each stage of the rotation with either four flowering shelves, using their own lamps set on 12-hour cycles, or one shelf divided into four areas.

When gardening with the SOG method, be aware that the setup requires you to have large numbers of plants in the rotation. This can cause you problems if the authorities discover the crop. They will base any fines or prison sentences on the potential value of your crop.

SOG plants are flowered after two weeks of vegetative growth, in pots or cubes spaced at 15cm between stems. It follows that the optimum sized container is a 15cm, square pot. The plants are either in potting compost for organic growers or in perlite, Golden Wool, coconut fibre or rockwool cubes for hydroponic feeding.

The first step for SOG production is to set out your growing spaces. For this technique you will require two separate grow rooms:

A. This grow room will be on a minimum of 18 hours of daylight and house the mother plants, the cuttings and the plants in *vegetative growth*. It will require two HPS lamps and a fluorescent setup for the cuttings.

B. This grow room will be on a strict 12-hour day/night cycle and will be the *flowering room*. It will house four crops at all times, but these will be in rotation. The crops take up the four corners of the room and need four separate HPS lamps.

A total of six HPS lamps will be required, plus fluorescents for the cloning table.

For illustration, we will assume that the grower wants to harvest around 250-grams of cannabis every two weeks. Using this method, the average yield per plant is between 7 and 14-grams of correctly cured buds, so this would require that approximately 20 plants be harvested every two weeks.

Room A

Set this room up first. In this example, we have chosen to use 600w HPS lamps with a small fluorescent table for our cuttings, but the lighting you choose will be dependent upon the size of your required crop.

Four mature females are required as mothers, to provide us with 20 cuttings every two weeks. These females are the first to be installed in pots containing your chosen medium and placed under the first sodium light. After two weeks, the first set of cuttings is taken. We take 25 to allow for any that fail to strike. The cuttings are placed under the fluorescent lights and will take two weeks to develop roots.

Two weeks later, we take 25 more cuttings to replace the original 25 that we have rooted under the fluorescents. Twenty of the newly rooted cuttings that were under the fluorescents are potted on into 15cm square pots containing your medium and moved under the second sodium lamp that has been set up in the pre-flowering area. The pots stand next to each other at 15cm between stems. Two weeks later we take a further 25 cuttings, and they replace the 25 that have rooted. Twenty of the newly rooted cuttings are potted on into 15cm pots and placed into the pre-flowering area. The twenty from the pre-flowering area are moved into *Room B* for flowering.

Room B

This room is set up with the remaining four sodium lamps, placed over four separate flowering areas. The twenty plants are now in area one under the *first* lamp.

Two weeks later we take 25 cuttings in Room A and they replace the 25 that have rooted. Twenty of the newly rooted cuttings are potted on into 15cm pots and placed in the pre-flowering area. The twenty from the pre-flowering area are moved into Room B for flowering under the *second* lamp.

Two weeks later we take 25 cuttings in Room A and they replace the 25 that have rooted. Twenty of the newly rooted cuttings are potted on into 15cm pots and placed in the pre-flowering area. The twenty from the pre-flowering area are moved into Room B for flowering under the *third* lamp.

Two weeks later we take 25 cuttings in Room A and they replace the 25 that have rooted. Twenty of the newly rooted cuttings are potted on into 15cm pots and placed in the pre-flowering area. The twenty from the pre-flowering area are moved into Room B for flowering under the *fourth* lamp.

Cannabis takes eight weeks to mature once it has been placed into flowering, so two weeks later we can harvest the plants from the first flowering crop, under lamp one, and that space can be filled with the next generation. This setup can continue indefinitely, giving you a crop every two weeks. The mothers may need replacing, so it is always a good idea to have a few extras in Room A. This technique works both organically and hydroponically and it is possible to build any of the active systems into the rotation. For most people, a floor and tray based setup is adequate, with the watering being carried out by hand. There is no limit to the size of this operation as extra lights can be added. Those who are growing smaller amounts can simply scale down and use smaller lamps or fluorescents.

Screen of Green (SCROG)

We touched on the Screen of Green (SCROG) technique in the mini/ micro cultivation section. It is covered in more depth here but the principles are basically the same. Screen of Green is not an intensive farming method like the SOG method but it produces excellent yields, and requires less plants in your grow room. A factor to consider when planning any cultivation as it will directly affect your punishment should the plants be discovered. The vegetative growth period is two weeks longer when using SCROG but you can expect yields of up to 80-grams per plant at a density of 1 plant per 30cm square.

A screen of chicken wire is suspended 30cm above your chosen planting medium and supported with either suspended chains from the ceiling, or posts around the grow table. Posts are most cultivators' first choice when building these systems, as chains have to be secured to the floor to stop any movement. A 600w HPS lamp will cover 1.5 square metres and produce fast growth. It follows that the optimum width of your screen will be around 60cm using these lamps. Using SCROG allows you to cultivate nine clones per metre. This area will yield more than 500-grams of dried buds, which more than compensates for any extra time spent in the vegetative stage.

To use SCROG commercially using 1,000w HPS you first prepare a long grow area 90cm wide and suspend your lamps centrally on lightrails spaced 90cm apart. The number you suspend is determined by the length of your SCROG run.

Once you have installed your lighting fixtures you can then set up the SCROG screen, which must be securely mounted. The best method of mounting depends on your grow location. Most growers build a flood and drain table with posts around the edge and the chicken wire is suspended horizontally between the posts. The frame should be 30cm above the top of your pots or cubes. It is also possible to build a SCROG run that is floor-based using CFS (see *p70*), the plants are secured to the underside of the wire as they develop, and are well supported by the screen, but it can be awkward stooping to tend the plants. Both hydroponic and organic cultivation methods can be incorporated into the SCROG run.

Place your clones into the SCROG run leaving approximately 30cm between stalks and working your way down the table. Then leave the plants to grow as normal with the same environmental conditions as recommended for any of the other systems. Between three and four weeks after being placed into the SCROG run, the plant tips will begin breaking through the wire mesh screen. Allow them to grow through by about 3cm and then pull them back through the screen and arrange them underneath, holding them in position with loose wire ties.

The flowering stage can now be started. Give the plants 12 hours of uninterrupted darkness each night cycle. Train the flower tops to fill the whole screen as they grow, and hold them loosely with ties. This doesn't affect growth, which can be over 3cm a day if you have optimum environmental conditions, so attend to the plants regularly at this stage. Any leaf growth that obscures the buds or comes through the screen is clipped back hard, along with all foliage and shoot growth between the growing medium and the buds wired underneath the screen. This area receives little light and the foliage will die back causing possible fungal infections. All that you should see under the screen are stems rising to a canopy of thick buds that are in optimum light conditions. If you have problems training the plant stems, crimp them slightly by bending them. The plant will recover quickly from crimping and continue growing with no ill effects.

You may need to tie down the middle of your screen as the plants push up against it and bend it towards the lights. Use nylon cord that can either be secured to the table or, if you are using an alternative cultivation technique such as CFS, you can tie weights to the end of the cord. Once growth slows, you have little maintenance to carry out on the screen. As long as the environmental factors are running at optimum levels you will be ready to harvest around eight weeks after inducing the flowering period.

Most growers try and utilize every lumen they can from their lamps, which makes economic sense. By creating vertical chicken wire screens around the sides of the growing table, in addition to the horizontal one, plants can be trained up and around the edge. This creates a box of foliage around your lights that is remarkable to see, but is more suited to the hobby grower. You can grow a *box of green* using a 70w HPS security light fitting; however, the sides tend to be sparse and thin. A mini system using a 250w HPS lamp is more effective, due to the extra output of lumens. Micro system growers are better off using a horizontal SCROG run with a reflective screen replacing the vertical wire. If you are growing commercially it can be time-consuming to construct boxes of green around your tables, but you may want to try it. Alternatively, replace the vertical wire with a reflective screen. There is plenty of light available from the 1,000w HPS, and it is uniformly distributed by the lightrails. Even on smaller setups utilizing 400w and 600w lamps there are still lumens being wasted.

The alternative to flat screen SCROG is to train plants vertically up the outside of the wire screens. Remove the lamp from its reflector and suspend it vertically, like a light bulb from a ceiling rose and arrange the screens in a box shape around it. Keep the bulb central and 20cm from the edge with larger lamps, and about 10cm in mini and micro systems. You will require an access point at the front for maintenance. Place the plants into your chosen growing medium, around the outside edge of each screen and train them up the sides. Place two plants per screen using 600w HPS lamps. An alternative to the box arrangement is the *tube of green*. Plants are grown on the outside of a tube of wire, with the lamp hung vertically in the centre.

All of the SCROG methods of cultivation can be incorporated into a rotation system similar to the SOG. The SCROG screens are in the flowering section and the area is divided to stagger the harvest. These screens are filled in rotation from a mother room nearby. The vegetative stage takes longer, so you are unable to crop every two weeks as you can with the SOG method; however, this is not a concern with most growers as the yield per plant ratio more than compensates for it. SCROG is an excellent technique for indoor cultivation as it ensures you supply optimum light levels to the flower tops at all times. This is a great advantage in smaller mini or micro setups, and for commercial farming it ensures a uniform and predictable crop.

Heavy Yielding Plants

Heavy yielding techniques require that you grow plants individually or in small numbers. The best yielding plants tend to be grown hydroponically and many growers use NFT, but it is possible to get good results using potting composts enhanced with growth promoters. You can also use oestrogen to boost plant growth if you want but it is not necessary for good results. Plants intended for heavy yield production are grown in very high light levels with one to four plants under 1,000w sodium in an air-cooled reflector, enabling the plants to be very close to the lamp. A reflective tent is built from bamboo canes wired together and covered with reflective sheeting, or alternatively a laundry drying rack can be used. The reflective tent completely surrounds the plants and lamp, ensuring that no light is wasted. The plants are allowed to establish themselves and develop a strong stem before they are defoliated. All of the leaves are stripped back, leaving just the branches. The plants are then regularly trimmed of large leaves right up until flowering: the leaves will start to grow back misshapen but this is normal. Once the plants reach a height of around 45cm the light cycle is changed to 12 hours and the plant is induced to flower. The flowering phase will take around 50 days.

Continual and severe defoliation produces what are known as polyploid plants: basically genetic mutations. Polyploidy is well known in the plant world and mutations can take many forms. What is of interest to the cannabis producer is that these mutations can produce abnormally high yields, although there is no increase in potency or THC content.

Polyploidy can be chemically induced in cannabis plants with colchicine which is found in crocus plants and can be extracted from the bulbs by crushing them. Dilute the juice with an equal amount of warm water and add a few drops of non-ionic wetting agent. Paint this solution onto the growing tips four times a day for three days; the plant will start to produce abnormal leaves that are misshapen and irregular. Although the colchicine has been extracted from a plant, it is poisonous and should be handled carefully wearing gloves.

If you do want to experiment with these plants it is easier to try to induce polyploidy by stripping the plant foliage back.

Secondary Budding

Cannabis plants grown under artificial light will flower when the daylight length is reduced from 18 plus hours to 12 hours. Buds start to appear along the females' growing tips, as flowers begin to form. After five weeks, while the buds are still immature but formed, secondary budding is induced by changing the day length to 24 hours of permanent daylight. This forces the plants back into the vegetative growth phase and fresh growing tips sprout from the newly formed buds. The flowers that were already forming will continue to grow, which has the effect of lengthening the area that is producing the bud.

The plant is grown on for a further four weeks before changing the light cycle back to 12 hours of uninterrupted darkness to induce flowering once more. The extra time required to flower your secondary bud crop is compensated for by a 25% increase in yield.

Pruning

Cannabis plants, when left alone, will reach heights in excess of 5 metres. This is obviously not practical for indoor cultivation so plants are kept short and bushy by pruning. Growing tips are pinched out of the young plants after they have developed their fourth set of leaves. The more you trim, the slower the plant grows, but this keeps the internodal length short and causes the plant to produce two new growing tips on either side of the injury. This is desirable for the cultivator as it means the plant will produce extra branches or 'leads'. Side shoots are similarly pinched out, along with any large fan leaves that may obscure light from the developing buds.

It is possible to produce five or more shoots from the pruned node by a little careful surgery on the growing tip. Instead of removing the complete tip in the conventional way where the whole node is cleanly removed, cut through the tip itself just below the centreline, aiming to leave around 10 to 15 % intact. The vegetation that is left contains rapidly dividing cells that will continue to form into shoots. Once flowering has started these shoots will also develop buds, increasing the density of top flowers.

It is not necessary to pinch out plants that are being cultivated in the SOG method as they will only produce one main cola, with little side shoot development, however, plants grown with more distance between centres should be trimmed, but can handle up to 10 leads, providing you maintain good light levels.

Ultra Violet Light

Cannabis plants produce more THC in response to receiving higher levels of ultra violet (UV) light. THC is thought to protect the plant from the harmful effects of sunlight. It is possible to reproduce this effect in the grow room environment by exposing the plants to 30 minutes of UV light during the day cycle. This exposure is usually divided into three 10-minute sessions. The UV light is delivered to the plants using sun bed tanning equipment. An area of two square metres will require 8 x 180cm long tubes.

Facial tanners can be utilized for smaller setups. Four x 30cm long tubes are used in conjunction with 400-watt lamps.

Regeneration

It is possible to harvest two, or even three, crops from your cannabis plants by a process known as *regeneration*. This is done by carefully harvesting only the top third section of your females. The lower section is removed from the flowering area and placed into a vegetative growth cycle. It is better to leave the females under a continuous light source for the first 10 days to speed up the reversion process, but they will revert under 18 hours of daylight.

Remove the buds from the ends of your plants' branches but leave all the fan leaves intact. It is important to leave as many of the smaller flowers on as possible, as these are the regeneration sites for new vegetative growth. The more flowers that are left on, the greater the potential for re-growth. The plant needs to be fed a high nitrogen growth formula feed. If you are cultivating hydroponically, this is easily done by switching from the bloom formulation to the required *grow* formula feed. If you are growing organic crops you should give the plant a weekly drench with seaweed extract and apply a 30-15-15 NPK fertilizer as a foliar spray. Some growers adjust the feeding of flowering females they want to regenerate well before harvest to ensure that the plants don't suffer from nitrogen deficiencies. It is important to have as many fan leaves on the plant as possible, so avoid any leaf pruning during vegetative growth.

Within 10 days of starting regeneration you should see signs of re-growth on the plant. The first vegetative growth may be misshapen but this is nothing to worry about, and future growth will appear normal. Once your plant has started growing back in the vegetative cycle, you will need to trim off any minor shoots and growth to allow the main stem to develop properly. Remove most of the lower vegetable material to ensure the plant's energy is directed into the main stems.

The plant can now be treated as normal and once it has established itself, placed back into the flowering room. A second harvest is possible in six to eight weeks after regeneration since the plant already has a strong stem and good root development. To regenerate the plant again, you follow the same procedure.

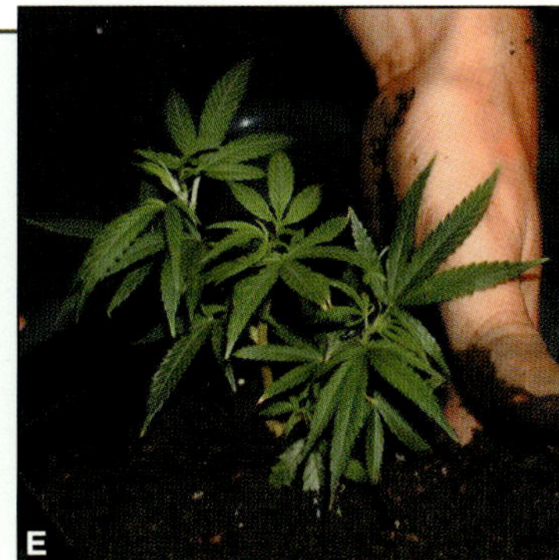

Cannabis sativa

(A) Seeds
(B) Seedling emerging
(C) First true leaves appear
(D) Vegetative growth begins
(E) Repotting young cutting
(F) Outdoor budding EU
(G) Outdoor vegetative growth EU
(H/H2) Polytunnel crops

Swiss Greenhouse

Shantibaba has produced most of the award-winning varieties of cannabis since 1990. These images taken at his facilities in Switzerland.

Good ventilation is essential to prevent mould developing

Shantibaba is the founder and breeder behind Mr. Nice Seedbank

Varieties

Cannabis indica and *Cannabis sativa* varieties are noticeably different. *C.sativa* plants grow taller and have thinner more angular leaves. *C.indica* plants are shorter with broad maple like leaves. Once flowering has been induced *C.indica* type plants produce thick flowers. *C.sativas* produce thick buds that are not as dense. There are hybrids available that combine the best traits of different cannabis varieties.

(A) Mature C.indica type with broad leaves
(B) C.indica x C.sativa hybrids develop denser buds than pure sativas
(C) Mature C.sativa type with narrow leaves

(A) Early flowering
(B) Pistils are emerging
(C) Pistils are evident
(D)+(E) Flower formation

Male and Female Cannabis Plants

(F) Hermaphrodite plant;
(1) Female (pistilate) and
(2) Male (staminate) flowers

(H) Pollen from male flowers

(G) Male flowers starting to open. Pollen is already being released

Taking Cuttings

Taking cuttings (cloning) from your plants is the best way to achieve consistent, all-female crops and is easy to do. Select a vigorous growing tip from a known female in the vegetative stage (A). Cut it from the plant (B) and either dip it into a rooting gel (C) and place the clone into a rooting medium such as rockwool starter cubes (E) or organic seed compost (F). Alternatively place the cutting into an aero-cloner with no nutrients or rooting compounds (D) where they will root in around 10 days with a 100% strike rate

Split tubes support the clones

Container has been left transparent to demonstrate the bubble effect. Ensure you lightproof any container you use

Rooting gel

E / F Rooted clones

Hydroponics in Holland

Powerplant in rockwool slabs

(A) View from above
(B) Healthy maturing buds
(C) Horizontal mesh support
(D) Powerplant is a heavy yielder
(E) Dense flower formation

Images courtesy Nol Van Shaik author of 'The Dutch Experience'

Nutrient Disorders

Healthy leaf

Nitrogen overdose

Nitrogen deficient

Phosphorus deficient

Potassium deficient

Magnesium deficient

Zinc deficient

Manganese deficient

Iron deficient

Sulphur deficient

Treat both nutrient overdose and deficiency by flushing the system through with fresh water and changing or adjusting the nutrient solution. Growers using compost mixes should leach the soil

Multiple overdose

Harvest

'Mr.Big' says bollocks!

(A) Close up of resin glands
(B+C) Ripe cannabis buds
(D+E) Buds are trimmed
(F) Pure herb/ no tobacco

Chapter 11

HARVESTING

I can resist everything except temptation. Oscar Wilde, 1854–1900

Indoor crops are harvested within 45 to 75 days, depending on the variety and cultivation method. Most indoor cannabis is Sinsemilla, or seedless, since fertilized buds are less potent and their weight is composed mostly of seed. The earlier you harvest your buds, the more THC they will contain. As the bud matures, it degrades THC into CBD and CBN, which gives cannabis less of a high and has a more lethargic affect on the user.

When 1/3 of the pistils have changed colour = More of a high
When 3/4 of the pistils have changed colour = Heavier smoke

Before you harvest female buds they should be pungent and glistening with a thick coat of translucent crystals. The false seedpods should appear to be bursting with resin and the tiny white pistil hairs protruding from the false seedpods should be brown or reddish and withering. The plant should be sticky and resinous to the touch. Check the buds under a magnifying glass and observe the individual glands: they should be covered with balls of resin. Finally, harvest a few selected buds and flash-dry them to correctly assess the quality of the crop. Choosing when to harvest is a matter of personal preference so experiment with your plants. Cut each plant at the base of the stem and remove it to your cool, dark drying room to prevent fungal attacks. Hang the plants upside down on a line and leave them to dry out slowly; the slower you dry out the flower heads the smoother the end product will be as chlorophyll, which gives cannabis its 'green taste', is removed through this slow curing process. Drying takes up to two weeks if the buds are to be properly cured, but applying a gentle heat to the drying area can speed up the process. Don't over-dry the buds.

They should give slightly when pressure is applied, and the stalk of each bud should crack when bent. However, over-dry buds will crumble and powder, so growers try to get the balance right. If you try to package your buds too wet they will begin to decay in the bags and quickly become ruined so ensure you dry your crop properly.

Correctly dried and cured cannabis contains around 15% moisture
Below 10% and the buds will be too brittle
Over 15% and they will be in danger from fungal spores

Hanging the plants has several advantages over drying them flat. Firstly, the small leaves that surround the flowers will dry around the buds, which help to protect the delicate *stalked capitate trichomes*. These tiny translucent structures are the glands that give the buds their frosted appearance and they contain the cannabinoid oils. These oils are chemicals unique to the cannabis plant and are collectively referred to by the name of the main psycho-active ingredient, THC. The larger leaves can later be trimmed away in a process known as manicuring.

Secondly, you are less likely to have fungal attacks since you can ensure that your drying room has good air circulation around the drying crop. Some growers place a small desk fan in the room to keep the air moving.

The third reason is aesthetic. Buds that have been dried hanging upside down appear more presentable. Most growers prefer to leave the buds in the shape they have dried, and this is by far the best way to ensure that none of the delicate glands that hold THC are knocked off or damaged. However, this is not practical if you are dealing with a large crop of buds, and if you need to transport any quantity you will have to compress the harvest to a certain size. Compressing is not ideal but is the best way to package buds for wholesale.

You don't need to make Dutch bricks that are shaped with a press, it is sufficient to just compact them by hand into resealable plastic bags.

If you are using vacuum packers or heat sealers to package your crop it can be compressed and shaped in the bags before sealing.

Smaller flowers can be made to look more presentable by compressing them by hand, or, if you have a large quantity, you can use a mould. Some growers make tubular moulds. The material is placed into a pipe that is held on a firm surface. A rod of a slightly smaller diameter is knocked into the open end with a hammer, compressing the buds. The tube is then turned over and the rod is struck onto a hard surface, pushing the compressed flower-tops out.

Others construct flat moulds from wooden frames that can be compressed in a vice, or in a small press constructed from three steel plates with holes drilled in each corner and four steel bars bolted to the top and bottom plates. The third plate slides in between them and a car bottle jack is used to drive it against the top plate. You can purchase presses that are designed for compacting old newspapers into bricks for the fire and they are ideal if you need to compress any quantity into a uniform size.

Commercial Dutch Skunk is nearly always compressed into half-kilo bales, to facilitate smuggling and it is usually packed fairly moist. Once it has been vacuum-sealed into polythene bags, the bales are wrapped tightly with parcel tape. This keeps the buds fresh and prevents fungal spores from forming. This technique doesn't give the end user the best deal: once opened the buds lose weight as they dry. The producers are trying to optimise their profits, but at least you know the buds haven't been tumbled to remove some of the THC. Many buyers lick their buds before a purchase; if they taste sweet it can indicate that they have been sprayed with a sugar solution in order to increase their weight.

Hashish prices have fluctuated in recent years and are considerably cheaper than in the past but Skunk, especially well dried and manicured Dutch varieties, is still holding its price – a reflection of its potency and quality.

Outdoor EU

(A) Early Skunk, pruned
(B) Holland's Hope
(C) Bonsai Shiva Skunk
(D) Early Skunk; No 1 choice for outdoor UK crops

(E) Holland's Hope in early flower

UK growers need to pick a mould resistant strain. Plants that are mainly *C.sativa* are not as mould resistant as *C.indica* varieties and suffer outdoors in wet weather

(F) Niagra. Heavy yielder but very prone to mould in UK

(G) Hotter parts of EU require a watering system. In the right location, UK growers can rely on adequate rainfall throughout the season. None of the UK plants pictured were watered

Chapter 11

OUTDOOR CROPS

Give me a spark of nature's fire, that's all the learning I desire. Robert Burns, 1759–1796

It is possible to grow cannabis outdoors even in Northern Europe where yields of up to 500-grams per plant can be achieved from *C.indica* plants. Crops are planted out after the last of the frosts, and are generally ready for harvesting in the last weeks of October. Unlike indoor cultivation, the grower has little control over the environmental factors that affect plant growth and depends on a good summer to harvest a high-yielding crop. However, cannabis is a hardy plant and, provided there are no frosts early in the season, and fungi, animals or parasites do not attack, it will give good yields.

C.sativa plants are not recommended for cooler climates within Europe although hybrids can perform well, especially in greenhouses. Pure sativas tend to grow tall and thin in the UK and Europe, yielding less than *Cannabis indicas* from the tougher *Hindu Kush* strain, which is less sensitive to cool weather. Try a good outdoor indica variety like the purpose-bred *Early Skunk,* which is very mould resistant*, Holland's Hope* or *Early Girl.* If these are not available, most *Cannabis indicas* will yield well outdoors even during a poor summer, but watch for mould during flowering. If you want to try a *Cannabis sativa* hybrid and the climate is not too damp, or you have access to a greenhouse use one of the hybrids available like Skunk#1 from Dutch Passion (25% Afghani, 25% Mexican Acapulco Gold and 50% Columbian Gold) or Niagra from Dr Greenthumbs in Canada.

Choosing Your Location

Finding a secure place to grow your outdoor crop of cannabis is the main problem you face as a cultivator. The distinctive shape and size of cannabis is easily recognizable, so you have to take steps to ensure the plants are not discovered. Drug crops do not need constant direct sunlight, five to six hours a day is sufficient, so try to screen the plants. When scouting for locations, look for areas where people do not go. Good outdoor locations include the following:

Outdoor locations

Cola forming Niagra UK
Heavy soil/2m in height/380g
mould problems later in
season

Greenhouses and polytunnels
Back yards (providing they are not visible to neighbours)
Gardens (as above)
Balconies (as above)
Rooftops (as above)
Scrubland and derelict areas
Parks (private areas can be found)
Farmland
Railway embankments
Motorway or highway embankments
Woodland clearings
Treetops (plants can be suspended in containers)
Military areas (crops have been cultivated behind no-go areas)
Riverbanks (once the tap root has grown down they won't require any watering)

UK growers can rely on good rainfall during the summer months. Choose an area that doesn't slope away from the plants as this will drain water from the grow area. Don't be put off if the area is heavy clay, it is possible to cultivate good crops in heavy soil and they retain more moisture than lighter, sandy soils. If you select your UK site well you can cultivate a crop without ever watering. Any foliar sprays you may use can be prepared away from the grow area and carried to the site in 5 litre spray bottles, which fit neatly into a walkers rucksack. If you can't carry sprays in, build a small well on the site. If the water becomes stale add some aquarium oxygenating tablets on each visit

When selecting your own location, remember it is better to grow large crops in an area that won't be linked back to you should they be discovered. Most cultivators spread their crop over several different locations, to ensure that at least some are harvested, and this is a good policy to adopt.

Try to find an area that has a water supply nearby. Carrying water in to the growing location can compromise the site and is hard work. In cooler areas of Europe like Holland, Germany and the UK growers only need to water younger plants during hot spells, as there is usually sufficient rainfall to sustain a crop. In warmer EU countries such as Portugal, Southern France and Spain growers have to supply additional water on a regular basis.

Preparing Your Location

Once you have found a suitable area in which to grow your plants you can start preparing it. Locate the crop in the most inaccessible part of the site; if there are brambles and thick undergrowth, cut an access path in and clear the centre. Ensure that the crop will receive as much light as possible by removing overhead foliage and branches. Always use the same track in and out of the growing area in order to avoid leaving obvious trails. Set warning traps on the approaches that will tell you if anyone has used your path. Try to use all the available cover to your advantage.

Be aware that if the authorities discover your crop they may mount an operation to catch you on your next visit.

Those growing in more remote locations need to construct some form of fencing to deter deer and rabbits from destroying the crop. The best fencing is plastic mesh netting that is cheap to purchase and light to carry. It can be secured around the edge of the intended growing space and acts as a barrier. When the crop is planted, additional protection is given to each plant by placing it into a 30cm long by 15cm diameter chicken wire sleeve that is supported on a short cane woven through the mesh. Once this is completed, work can begin on improving the soil.

Soil Types

Soil was formed millions of years ago from rock that was powdered by the actions of wind, rain, and frosts eroding its surface. Some types of soil are formed directly from the rocks underneath their surface; others were deposited by the wind. Freshly formed soil has all the elements that were in the original eroded rock, but it requires a vital addition in the form of decayed living matter, known as humus, in order for it to support plant life.

Soil comes in many varieties due to the differences in the rocks that are broken down in its formation, so it's not always possible to get the correct soil type for your crop.

Soil is categorized as being either light or heavy.

Light

Light soil is composed of large particles. Sand is the lightest soil, and you can see the individual particles.

Heavy

Heavy soil is composed of the smallest particles. Clay is the heaviest soil. The definition of heavy or light doesn't refer to the weight of the soil but to the ease with which it can be worked.

Beneath the surface topsoil is another layer known as the subsoil. This tends to be humus-free but rich in minerals providing a balanced nutrient supply for those plants, such as cannabis, that can root deeply enough to reach it.

Soil is further categorized by type.

Peat Soil

Peat soils are formed under water from compressed, decomposed plant material. They are only found in specific areas; however, if they can be located they are ideal for cultivation but can be acidic.

Sandy Soil

Sandy soils require large amounts of organic material and manure to make them suitable for cannabis growth. They tend not to hold water, so they need monitoring to ensure they don't dry out.

Loam Soil

Loam is a mixture of clay and sand. Well-fertilized loam soils are ideal for cannabis cultivation.

Clay Soil

Well-drained clay soils are suitable for cannabis crops; however, care must be taken to ensure they don't become waterlogged. Most can be improved with manure and soil treatments.

Identifying Your Soil Type

The best test for soil type is to dig out a section of earth and compress it in your hand. Heavy soil will form into a mass, whereas lighter soils will crumble. Pull the sample apart between your fingers and observe the colour and texture and look to see if it is sandy, clay, or dark and peat-like. Soil analysis is based on the quantities of nutrients contained in any given sample, and it is possible to get an accurate indication of the quality of your soil by using a test kit. Some growers send their samples to be analysed by a laboratory analysis service, which provides an extremely accurate picture of the soil's macro and micronutrient content.

The pH level is also important, and you can use either a dip test or a probe that is pushed into the ground and gives an instant reading of the pH.

Examine the soil for pests and weeds. Leather jackets, the maggots of the European Crane fly, and wireworms are obvious to spot in your sample digs. It is not feasible to examine the soil for disease by using pathological plating and incubation tests so growers need to check the surrounding foliage for signs of any disorders. If the plants show signs of damage or wilting you could have a problem.

Once the soil has been analysed you can remedy any shortfalls by adding fertilizer or manure to the area. There is no requirement to dig the soil over. It is a common misconception that soils need to be turned. For light soils, a no-dig approach is actually better for the soil. Digging speeds up the breakdown of organic matter in the soil, which is to be avoided.

Add fertilizers by spreading them over the surface, and allow them to be absorbed by the soil. Many growers used concentrated bone meal fertilizer on outdoor gardens as it has the added effect of deterring deer and rabbits. However, since the outbreak of vCJD (Mad Cow Disease) in Europe there have been concerns about its use. Bone meal is made from the spinal cords of carcasses, the high-risk area for the infectious agent that causes the disease. Infected carcasses could find their way into processing plants and you could put yourself at risk when inhaling and handling the fertilizer. Instead, use chicken manure pellets, or fresh manure if it's available to you. Alternatively, if the soil is particularly poor, use a slow release, granular chemical fertilizer and follow the manufacturer's recommendations for surface dressing. We are looking for a balanced NPK reading but unlike growing indoors this isn't an exact science. As long as the soil is well drained and healthy we can supply the remaining nutrients on a regular basis with foliar feeding to the plant leaves. The same fertilizers that are recommended for organic indoor cultivation are suitable for outdoor growing.

Some cultivators choose not to grow their plants directly in the soil and use growbags, pots, or plastic bags filled with potting compost. These work well, especially for smaller setups in back yards and on balconies. But containers require watering regularly, whereas mature plants in the ground with a well-established root system and deep tap root can survive on their own for longer periods. Only plant one or, at most, two plants into a growbag outdoors.

It is possible to grow outdoor crops hydroponically. Many growers also use these systems in greenhouse setups, and they produce consistently high yields. It is easy to set up a small hydroponic unit outside if you want, and any one of the active or passive setups described in the hydroponics section will work well.

Preparing Your Crop

Cannabis grown from seed that has not been feminised will produce a crop that is composed of approximately 50% each of both males and females. This is undesirable for cannabis cultivators, especially outdoors where large crops are easily compromised. A crop of known females can be half the size of an indeterminate crop and still yield the same amount of bud. Cultivation in the cooler areas of Europe and Switzerland is mostly carried out using clones that have been prepared indoors at the beginning of March. The clones are given two weeks to root and are then transferred to peat pots filled with fine potting compost and put in a greenhouse or on a window ledge to harden off. The greenhouse can be a simple construction made from polythene sheeting. During the first weeks of April the clones are placed outdoors during good weather and brought back inside every evening. By mid April, or after the last frosts and when the young plants have reached a height of 15 to 20cm, they are packed into cardboard boxes and transferred to the growing area. This is best done at night, but it depends on your location. Tape a larger plant pot over the top of each clone, to protect it during transit.

The alternative to using cuttings is to germinate your seedlings earlier and place them in a greenhouse or on a window ledge to harden. The same procedure is carried out as is used for the cuttings; however, as soon as the plants are between 5 and 10cm tall they are forced into the flowering stage by giving them 12 hours of uninterrupted darkness every night cycle. To do this, place them in a specially prepared darkened area or, in the case of a few plants, into a box. Within two weeks they will begin to exhibit signs of gender. After two weeks, remove the young plants from the flowering cycle, even if they are indeterminate (not showing gender). The plants will continue to flower as they revert back to the vegetative state, and can easily be identified. If you want to keep a male, select the strongest plant and cut it back hard. Remove the forming male flowers, and only leave a few lower shoots. Male plants die soon after flowering so it is important to encourage fresh vegetative growth.

Within a few weeks of removing your females from the flowering cycle, they will be growing back in the vegetative state without any ill effects. If you are prepared well in advance of the growing season, bring your plants on indoors under artificial light. You don't need any specialized horticultural lamps, seedlings respond perfectly well to a 100-watt incandescent household light bulb. Position an adjustable desk lamp over the plants, keeping it as close as possible without burning the leaves. You will be surprised at the results.

The third method of gender identification involves growing your seedlings on until a cutting can be taken from each of them. The cutting and plant are each labelled to identify the mother and clone, and the cuttings are rooted and flowered. It's possible to root the cuttings under 12 hours of daylight, which will save you two weeks. The mother plants are grown on either in the greenhouse, or taken to the grow area, but they are kept in containers until their sex is determined. Once they have flowered, you can trace the parent plant and, if it is male, remove it.

You can also identify the sex of your plants by selectively flowering a lower branch. Cover a branch for 12 hours every 24 hours with a sleeve made from black sugar paper, which blocks out light but still allows the plant to breath. (Covers made from plastic will create the perfect environment for fungal attacks, so avoid using them.) Within two weeks the plant will begin to show signs of gender.

Planting Out

Cannabis, when grown outdoors, can grow very tall. Depending on your situation, it is best to prune your plants to keep them short. However, you will want to encourage thick, bushy side growth, so spacing of the individual plants is important. Plants that are crowded and competing for light will grow tall and thin with little side shoot development.

Plant out your female crop at a one-metre distance between stems. Pacing a large step between plants will help you measure out that distance. Dig a hole with a trowel and, if you only have a small number of plants, add a handful of water-absorbing crystals of the type normally used in hanging baskets. This practice will assist the young plant by giving it a small reservoir of water, but it can work out to be expensive in large operations. The plants are then watered in and, if it is a wildlife area, a sleeve of chicken wire is placed over each clone, and a cane threaded through it. The young plants will need watering regularly until they have developed a strong root system.

You can water your crop by hand with containers or Jerry cans that you bring from your water source. If there is a river nearby and the situation allows, crops can be watered using a small petrol-driven pump. The types used in the construction industry for pumping out ditches are excellent and can be hired or acquired. If you don't have a nearby water supply, dig a hole and line it with a polythene tarpaulin. Cover the top with more polythene pegged out and weighted with a stone in the middle. Bury the polythene edges or you could trap small mammals, which are beneficial slug and insect predators. Pierce the centre of your rain trap with a few small holes and leave the well to fill up naturally. In some areas you will only need to water the plants as they establish themselves and can rely on rainfall during the season.

Foliar feeding is best carried out with a horticultural backpack sprayer, using the fertilizers recommended (see *p51*) the same sprayer can be cleaned and used for treatment sprays. Take care not to overfeed your plants. It is better to use a diluted application of foliar feed and watch how the plants respond. Remember that younger crops require less feed than mature or budding plants.

Foliar feeds should be combined with a surface dressing of either chicken manure or granulated fertilizer that is sprinkled around each plant at the recommended rate (which depends on the feed you've chosen). Lightly fork the fertilizer into the soil around each plant, ensuring that the area under the branches is evenly covered, and water it well in. Two weeks before flowering, give the area a light surface dressing of sulphate of potash. This encourages better flower formation and resistance to disease. Three weeks after planting out you need to weed the plot to remove any wild plants that may be competing. Only clear an area around the plant itself, as you need vegetation to give you cover, and weeds help the soil to retain moisture. You will need to repeat this again as more weeds develop.

Disguising Your Plants

Cannabis is easily identifiable so hide and disguise your plants to avoid them being spotted, especially when growing plants in your back yard or on balconies. Pruning your crop will develop short and bushy plants, and this should be your first step. Pinch out the growing tips when the plants are short and keep them small during the vegetative growth phase. Try starting your plants later in the season so they will be smaller and remove or trim some of the larger, more distinctive fan leaves. Some growers bend the top of the plant over and tie it down to allow the side shoots to grow upwards, which gives the appearance of a row of mini plants rising from the main stem. Plastic flowers and fruit can also be attached to the plant to disguise it further: wire them on with gardening wire.

Some growers train their plants along a trellis that is fixed to a south-facing wall in much the same way as vines are grown. Alternatively, pinch out the growing tip when the plant reaches 30cm and grow the two new side shoots out horizontally, in either direction of the trellis. Cut back any unwanted growth. The side shoots will grow out quite a distance and artificial flowers or fruit can also be attached as a further disguise. These plants are strange to look at but actually produce quality buds as the flowers receive good levels of unshaded sunlight.

Plants can also be trained to grow along the ground. Just pinch out the growing tip at the third internode and then train the new tips to grow sideways by wiring them down to either side of the cannabis plant. Trim and wire new growth as it develops. You are not limited to two side shoots; many growers have them going in four directions. These plants need protection from pests and insects such as snails and slugs, and tend to produce small yields. However, they can be effectively grown along the fronts of balconies with the plant rooted in a growbag and the branches held down with weighted cord.

Treetop Cultivation

The more agile farmer may be interested in cultivating a crop high in the treetops. Plants grown this way receive optimum sunshine but are left exposed to any unexpected bad weather, so a good crop is dependant on a fine summer. The plants are grown in large 30 to 40 litre plastic containers that are spray painted green and brown, and covered with ripped sacking or camouflage netting to resemble foliage.

This disguises the plants from the ground. The containers are then filled with equal quantities of potting compost and perlite mixed 50-50 with coconut fibre or rockwool granules. Or, if you can obtain a sufficient quantity, use water-absorbing crystals. Plant a single female in each container, water it well, and tape a polythene lid around the top to prevent evaporation. Then hoist the containers up into the branches and lash them into position. Some growers like to build platforms in the canopy to create a cannabis treehouse, holding several plants.

Safety is a factor when watering your treetop plants and it is advisable to invest in a pair of rubber soled climbing boots, a harness, and some quality climbing rope. Secure rings into the trunk that you can attach yourself to. Hoist water up in containers when the plants need it, which can be weekly when they are mature, and also during hot weather. Towards the end of the growing season you will lose a lot of cover as the trees shed their leaves, so you will need to position your plants fairly high up in the canopy and ensure that they are difficult to see from the ground.

Greenhouse Cultivation

Greenhouses and polytunnels offer the outdoor cultivator a protected environment in which to grow that can be controlled to a certain extent by the use of fans, heaters and even horticultural lighting. Lamps can be installed to supplement natural light and will make up for any shortfalls in the season. Greenhouse cultivation can be either hydroponic or utilize compost in containers, although for larger polytunnel setups planting directly into the soil is preferable. Cannabis plants will strip any ground they are planted into and heavy fertilization is required to bring the soil back for the next season's crop. Plants grown in greenhouses can be forced into early flower production quite easily by reducing their exposure to daylight. Use covers to block out the light.

Greenhouse Grow Rooms

An alternative to greenhouses and polytunnels is to convert a shed or outbuilding into a grow area by removing the roof and replacing it with glass or plastic panels. Disguise the panels with white greenhouse shading paints if the area is visible from other buildings. The walls of the grow room are lined with reflective material. Warm white fluorescent tubes are installed along the walls to add a low-cost supplement to the natural sunlight and ensure good growth on the bottom branches of the plants. Only run the lights during daylight hours to avoid compromising the setup. Use fans to recirculate and cool the air, and in southern climates use air conditioners to prevent heat build up. In colder climates heat is generated from fuel-burning greenhouse heaters that also release CO_2.

The plants can be grown both organically and hydroponically. In some buildings it's possible to remove the floor and plant directly into the underlying earth, but it is better to dig out the original soil and replace it with potting compost each season using specially constructed holes for each individual plant. It is easier to use a hydroponic floor-based setup such as CFS rather than digging out your planting areas. A floor-based setup will produce crops as good as if not better than the earth grown system, but it depends on your situation and location. Some medical cannabis users are physically unable to do the digging and lifting required and an automated hydroponic system is the ideal solution.

Daylight Reduction

Just as you force the young plants to flower earlier in the season to determine their gender, you can also force outdoor crops to flower for an early harvest by giving them 12 hours of uninterrupted darkness. Most growers will do this in the late summer when the plants have already benefited from the best of the sunshine and are strong and healthy.

Forcing the flowering can be labour intensive as plants need moving or covering on a daily basis. However, it is worth the effort as your plants can be flowering early and producing their buds in good levels of sunshine. Plants grown in containers are easier to force as they can simply be moved into a lightproof area for the 12-hour period. Plants that are in the ground need covering, which sometimes causes heat buildup problems, so shading is usually started in the evenings. You need to build a frame around the plant so that the cover can be easily placed without touching the plant leaves. This is especially true if you are using polythene covers as they can cause the foliage to become damaged and wet, leading to fungal infections. Use either thick black polythene or black/white polythene as your cover and ensure the edges are light proofed by securing all joins with masking tape. Alternatively, large cardboard boxes can be waterproofed and used.

A Ton of Skunk

Two thousand female *Cannabis indica* skunk plants, if successfully cultivated and harvested, even in cooler climates, will yield approximately 1000 kilos or 1 ton of dried buds. The area required to cultivate 2,000 plants with 1 metre between each one is an area roughly 50 paces long by 40 paces wide. Have the soil tested professionally and adjust it if necessary. The easiest way is with chemical fertilizer spread by hand or machine. You don't have to plough the field, but the weeds need to be cut back and left as mulch on the surface. You will have to repeat this at regular intervals to ensure that nothing competes with the crop. Don't use weed killers, you need some cover to retain moisture in the soil, and cannabis, once established, will outgrow any local wild plants. The area will need some form of fencing with mesh or wire in order to deter wildlife.

First you'll need to prepare your seed stock - double the amount to account for the males, unless you have access to a large quantity of feminised seeds or enough mothers to supply you with 2,000 cuttings. Many growers prefer to use seed, preferably F1 hybrids (see *p123*), and this is done either indoors, with a crop that is flowered and fertilized, or by preparing well in advance and growing an outdoor seed crop the previous season. When farming on this scale using indeterminate seeds, try the feminising treatments (see *p45*) to increase the female to male ratio by about 20%. You will need to germinate over 4,000 seedlings in the first week of March, which is very labour intensive. However, with proper organization it is manageable. Weigh 100 seeds using digital jewellers' scales; you can then calculate your number of seeds by weight.

Germinate your seedlings in trays of vermiculite and, as they appear over the next week to ten days, transfer them to 10cm plastic pots filled with seed-grade potting compost. Place these pots into a greenhouse or polytunnel and allow the seedlings to grow on. When they reach a height of 8 to 10cm, force them to flower by giving them 12 hours of uninterrupted darkness. This is best done by growing the young plants on carts or trolleys that can be wheeled into and out of your flowering shed. To use a polytunnel for the forcing, cover it with black, lightproof plastic as they do at mushroom farms. It is better to have two polytunnels facing each other, end to end, one for flowering and one for growth. The plants can then be wheeled between the two. You'll need a generator to run fans but propane burners, which will also give off CO_2 can supply heat if needed.

Within two weeks the gender of the plants can be identified and the females placed permanently into vegetative growth and the males discarded. When the females are 20 to 30cm in height, transfer them to the grow area. Start in the far corner and pace out the spacing, work in a grid leaving 1 metre between plants, and dig a small hole for each one. Then transport the plants 50 at a time, in a wheelbarrow. Remove them from their pots and plant them. Provide water from your source using pumps or hoses and support the plants with fencing wire or thick cord stretched horizontally between 1-metre posts along each row.

Treatments and feeding can be carried out with a horticultural backpack sprayer combined with regular, dried fertilizer applications to the area under each plant. Harvest the crop in late October and dry it in the forcing shed before manicuring and compressing it into 500-gram bales for vacuum packing.

The Swiss authorities allow the cultivation of cannabis plants, and nurseries there grow potent skunk plants. However, cultivators prefer to grow mother plants in greenhouses with additional horticultural lighting to ensure that they stay in the vegetative stage. Cuttings are taken and rooted, then later planted out or placed into greenhouses, where they are grown both hydroponically and organically with reduced spacing between individual plants. By reducing the plant's daylight and using HID lighting it is possible to produce several crops in rotation. This is a good, intensive way to farm cannabis but requires a large nursery setup, whereas the Ton of Skunk method is low-tech, requiring only a forcing shed and, if possible, a polytunnel.

Harvesting Your Outdoor Crop

The same principles apply to outdoor and indoor crops when it comes to assessing the readiness of your harvest. If you are unsure, harvest a few select buds and sample them. If you intend to sell the crop, wait until they are at their heaviest, which can mean that some of the THC has been degraded into CBD and CBN's. With practice, you will be able to judge when the plants have a good balance of THC and material weight. Harvesting in remote locations is better carried out at night, but it depends on your situation. Trim down the plants using pruning shears or a sharp machete. Cut off each individual branch and then the main stem and lay them on a plastic sheet. When you have collected the crop, the sheet can be rolled and tied neatly; the harvest is then removed to a safe area for drying.

If you only have a small amount of buds then dry the branches by hanging them from a line in a darkened, cool area. If you have a larger crop it is better to clip the buds from the branches and trim the leaves off while they are still wet. The buds can then be hung on a line or dried flat on newspaper, but ensure you turn them regularly. Allow the buds to dry out slowly, which will remove most of the chlorophyll and give a smoother, better tasting harvest. Ensure that you don't over-dry the buds. The small stalks should be brittle to the touch but the bud needs to have a slight elasticity. Buds that are too dry will crumble and disintegrate when packed.

Store your dried buds in a cool dark place. Seal them into plastic bags and then cover the bags with parcel tape. Light can encourage both decomposition and the growth of fungal spores.

If you are dealing with any quantity of cannabis buds it is a good idea to invest in a small heat-sealer and some lay-flat plastic tubing. You make the bags up from the tubing by heat-sealing each end and cutting it from the roll. Place a small piece of newspaper in with the buds to absorb any moisture and don't try to pack them too wet, as they will deteriorate rapidly.

Heat-sealers can be bought for a reasonable price. Check your phone book for packaging wholesalers or local kitchen equipment retailers as there are units designed to assist you in home freezing that work well. You can use heat-sealing equipment to give you a form of vacuum packing that helps preserve your harvest by first sealing the buds into a tightly fitting bag. Apply pressure to the bag once it has been sealed and force any trapped air into one corner. Then pierce that corner with a pin and force the air out of the bag. While you still have pressure on the bag, get an assistant to place a small piece of clear, waterproof adhesive tape over the pinhole. The buds are now sealed in a vacuum. You can purchase the tape from garden centres where it is sold to repair greenhouses and polytunnels.

In the unlikely event that you need to store any buds they can be placed in the refrigerator without any risk of deterioration. Don't freeze your harvest as the freezing process damages the delicate stalked capitate trichomes. They become brittle and break off, affecting the potency of your buds. Store your personal supply in a lightproof box. Single buds can be carried in waterproof plastic money tubes, like those worn around your neck on the beach. Alternatively, compress the buds in a plastic bag and then wrap them in parcel tape.

Chapter 13

BREEDING

In nature there are neither rewards nor punishments, only consequences. Ingersol.

At some point you may decide to breed from your favourite plants. Cuttings will only produce genetic replicas of the mother and, although this is fine for the purpose of cultivation, it prevents any natural development of your stock. By selecting a female with outstanding traits, you can pollinate her using a strong, well formed male either from the same variety or, better still, from one of the many others that have traits you want to incorporate into your stock.

It is important to define what breeding actually means. Many growers cross varieties and then clone the best examples for their gardens. Although this is a good way to develop certain traits in your harvest, it does not provide you with a true breeding strain of plant. To develop a new strain you need to stabilize the hybrids by inbreeding the stock, which allows you to produce consistent chromosomes and establish common characteristics.

It is better to keep your males and females apart when breeding but if that is not possible, remove the males from the grow room as soon as they have been identified. Males do not need much light once they have started to flower but you must keep them in a 12-hour light cycle. Place the plant on a sheet of clean paper in an area that has no air circulation. The pollen will fall on the paper, and can be collected by folding the paper in half and pouring the contents neatly into a test tube or vial. Alternatively, you can cut off a healthy branch and place the stalks in a glass of weak sugar and water solution. Then stand the glass on a sheet of clean white paper and collect the pollen. You can further harvest the pollen by holding a sheet of paper under the flowers and tapping them gently with a pencil. If the flowers themselves fall onto your collection paper, pick them out and discard.

The pollen is then diluted in a 'carrier', usually flour that has been microwaved for at least five minutes. Once the flour has cooled, it can be added to the pollen you have collected. Only one pollen cell is needed to fertilize a single female ovule, so using a carrier reduces waste.

Add half a teaspoon of pollen to 4 teaspoons of sterilized flour and store the mixture in an airtight vial. Test tubes are most breeders' choice for storing pollen, and a hobby chemistry set will provide you with ample supplies. Try to get tubes with plastic stopper lids rather than corks. Label the tubes with details of the male plant and date them. If you intend to store your pollen for any length of time, keep it refrigerated and it should last for a few months.

It is possible to keep a male cannabis plant alive indefinitely by cutting it back hard, once it has flowered. If you need to delay the onset of flowering in your male plant, you can shock it by crimping its top over.

When you have selected the female you want to breed from, simply take one of your test tubes into the flowering area. Use a small artist's brush and dip the tip into your tube, then gently stroke the brush over the fine white pistils on selected flowers. The flowers will be most receptive to pollination two weeks after the flower clusters have formed. The seeds will take between four and six weeks to fully develop and they are not harvested until they have a dark, speckled appearance and seem to be bursting from the pods. The branches are cut and allowed to dry for about ten days. The seeds can then be picked out by hand and stored in labelled airtight containers. They are best kept in a refrigerator for long-term storage.

When choosing your parent plant for breeding purposes, you need to carefully examine the traits of the individual plants, since they are the gene pool of your future generations. Growers can have different requirements from their stock based on environmental growing conditions and the cultivation techniques they choose. The general rule when selecting stock plants is to choose those that grow and mature the fastest. Once you have identified these plants you can then further categorize them by potency and yield. If you are growing outdoor crops in cooler climates you may want to introduce a certain amount of frost resistance to your stock. By carefully selecting your varieties you can develop this and many other desirable traits. When you cross two different varieties of cannabis plants, the resultant offspring are known as hybrids. These hybrid plants will all be very different from each other. Seeds from the same plant will all exhibit different traits, so it is important to grow a wide selection to maturity in order to examine them for vigour and potency. The best examples are then kept for further breeding. It is better to breed from two plant varieties that show contrastingly different traits. In this way you create what is referred to as 'hybrid vigour' and the resultant offspring will exhibit a good selection of the genes of both parents. The first generation of two genetically different, but true breeding and stabilized plants, are called F1 hybrids, and they grow 25% faster and bigger than any other crosses. The offspring of F1 hybrids are called F2, their offspring are F3, and so on, however, these generations after F1 will not exhibit hybrid vigour.

If the plants you have selected to breed from both contain dominant genes for certain characteristics or traits, then the resultant offspring will display either one or the other these traits. This makes it difficult to combine characteristics from the two parents, as the offspring will only exhibit the dominant trait of one plant. You can overcome this difficulty by inbreeding the seeds from the first cross. This means growing the seeds to maturity and pollinating a female with a male from the same batch. In this way, recessive genes become magnified and available, and the new seeds will exhibit a better balance of the traits you are looking for. Inbreeding is a necessary, but not desirable, practice for producing new stock since it means continually drawing from the same gene pool. Some recessive traits may become prevalent that can reduce potency and vigour. However, to produce true breeding plants you need to backcross your females with males from the same strain. It is important to keep records of your plants and their progress. Many breeders photograph and catalogue their stock but there are security implications if the police discover these records, and it will be used against you in any subsequent court appearances to demonstrate your professionalism and intent.

Feminised Seeds

It is possible to produce seeds that have no male chromosomes in their genetic make-up and therefore, when germinated, produce all female plants. This is desirable to the cannabis cultivator for several reasons; the main one being that it is difficult to select males to breed from. Although it is possible to assess the male's vigour and speed of growth, it is not possible to assess its potency since they do not produce any buds. It becomes a process of trial and error which, when considering the penalties imposed for possessing cannabis plants, is undesirable. Cultivators should seek consistent results from as few plants as possible to minimize their risk. Feminised seeds solve this problem by allowing you to select two females with known characteristics and use them as your gene pool.

Gibberellic Acid

When applied to female cannabis plants, gibberellic acid causes them to develop male flowers in the treated area. This technique allows us to collect viable pollen from a female plant. The acid is readily available from horticultural wholesalers, and is used by nurseries for plant breeding and hybridisation. Spray a few of the upper branches of your chosen female every day for 14 days with a 100 ppm solution. Add a few drops of non-ionic wetting agent to your gibberellic acid solution to improve uptake in the plant. Once your female has flowered you can collect the pollen or simply remove the branches for later collection, as described earlier. The second female, which will carry the seeds, can then be pollinated. Since there are no male chromosomes present in the pollen used for the fertilization, the resulting seeds will all be female. Some varieties are better suited than others for this technique so you will need to experiment with your plants.

It is possible to pollinate the female treated with the gibberellic acid with its own male flowers, in effect crossing it with itself. This process can be used to preserve desirable plants but there is a danger of loss of vigour due to inbreeding. There are some mail order seed suppliers who stock feminised seeds, check out the website for more details.

Strains from around the world...

Afghani
Pure variety from Afghanistan, never hybridized. Very broad leaves, 100% Indica. Heavy resinous buds. Some plants turn purple at harvest time. High flower to leaf ratio. Aroma and flavour are heavy. Very strong, narcotic high. Average yields. Specifications: Flower: 8-9 weeks ~ Harvest: 1st week of Nov.

Bushman
Indica/Sativa. This strain comes out of the Australian bush, full fruity flavour and an "up" sativa stone. Flowering time 9 to 10 weeks. Harvest end of Oct

California Orange
A stabilized hybrid, inbred since 1980. Can be extremely resinous, including the leaves. 50% Sativa, 50% Indica. Pronounced citrus aroma and flavour. Very strong, fairly clear high. Yields are slightly above average. Specifications: Flower: 8-10 weeks ~ Harvest: 1st week of Nov.

Chitral
Variety of the famous Chitral-hasj of the 70's. Hybridized with Skunk, now even stronger. Good harvest, herbal taste and strong "physical high". Specifications: ~ Flower: 8 weeks ~ Harvest: 3rd week of Oct.

Colombian Gold
Indica/Sativa. From Bogota, large dense colas and huge resin glands. From cuttings plants can be flowered for 65-75 days and be fully developed. Hash taste. Flowering time 9 to 11 weeks.

Durban Poison
Exclusively inbred, never hybridized, 100% Sativa. Large long bud leaves, buds are also large and long with lots of resin. A sweet licorice or aniseed flavour. "Up" high similar to Thai. High yields. Well suited for out crossing with late bloomers to produce earlier flowering. Also does very well under artificial light. Specifications: ~ Flower: 8-9 weeks ~ Harvest: end of Sept.

Ethiopian Highland
Sativa. Considered the finest in the world by the ruling Empress Zauditu and Ras Tafari who became the Emperor Haile Selassie. Cultivated and inbred by his latter day followers in the city of Shashemene, this sativa grows well at altitude and in cooler climates. Buds typically long sativa with visible resin droplets providing a clear energetic high. Plants are shorter, branched and stockier than the tall bushy southern African types. Height 4.5 to 6 ft. Flowering time 8 to 12 weeks. Yield 500 gm.

Golden Triangle Thai
Sativa. From the wild jungles of Thailand. Mellow high with a lemon flavour. Height 10 feet. Flowering time 16 weeks. Veg 1 wk for sea of green. Yield 6oz (168g) full size. 1/2oz (14g) in 2 gal. pot. Harvest outdoor End of Dec

Hindu Kush
Pure Indica, one of the most constant kind. Best start for anyone who wants to grow his own Indica. Hash like taste, large firm buds, good yield. Specifications: ~ Flower: 8 weeks

Lambsbread
Jamaican speciality. A very special taste and high. Grows with long slim buds. 100% Sativa.

Malawi Gold
High yields from large resinous buds loaded with THC. Heavy stoned high, strong flavour.

Skunk#1
(75% Sativa, 25% Indica) was originally a cross between 25% Afghani, 25% Mexican Acapulco Gold and 50% Colombian Gold. Inbred since 1978, now a stabilized homogeneous strain.

Thai
This is a pure sativa that yields large buds and the typical Thai flavour. Because of the long maturity stage, this variety isn't for everyone and is useless outdoors in EU. Matures in 70-100 days. Energetic, clear high.

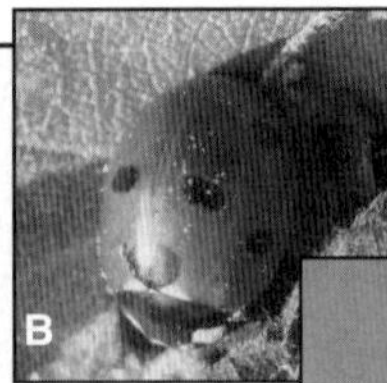

(A) Overfertilized plant shows curled, misshapen leaves
(B) Ladybird
(C) Hoverfly
(D) Leaf damage UK outdoor
(E) This caterpillar feeds on the plant before cocooning itself within a smaller leaf
(F) Spider mite infested buds
(G) Spider mite infested leaf

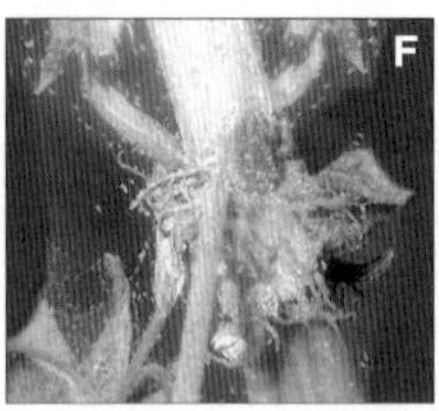

Spider mites

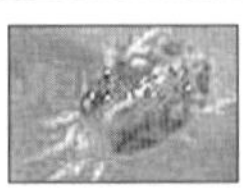

Spider mite life cycle of egg, nymph, two nymph moults and adult life takes place in under a month. Treat infestations with Pyrethrum spray or Neem oil at the first sign of attack / repeat weekly for 5 weeks to kill any eggs remaining

Chapter 14

PESTS AND FUNGI

There's a sucker born every minute. P. Barnum, 1845.

Both indoor and outdoor cannabis crops are attacked by the same insect pests and suffer from the same fungal infections. However, these problems become magnified in an indoor environment. Humidity can rise to unacceptable levels encouraging fungal infections, and parasitic insect attacks are worse since the conditions are perfect for breeding pests. Spider mites are by far the most damaging of insect pests and although they can be controlled with both insecticides and predator mites, the first rule for all indoor and greenhouse gardeners should be that prevention is better than cure. Keep areas clean at all times, remove any plant trimmings, and in larger setups, invest in an industrial-grade vacuum cleaner that can suck up water spills. Vacuum the area regularly, paying attention to edges and corners. Wash surfaces and sterilize your equipment with a dilute solution of hydrogen peroxide (H_2O_2). A 17.5% solution is diluted at the rate of 5mls per litre of water, or you can use a 5% dilute bleach solution. Indoor and outdoor growers should spray crops with a preventative systemic fungicide every two weeks during flowering and humid conditions, using a treatment that contains carbendazime, a chemical that is recommended for fruit and vegetable treatment. Use the recommended application for tomatoes and stop spraying at least ten days before harvest. Ensure that all vents are filtered through ladies' stockings or pantyhose, since the fine mesh will trap flying insects. Never enter your grow areas after working in outdoor gardens or walking through locations with other plants and foliage. Some growers remove their outer clothes and wear paper coveralls in their growing areas to avoid cross contamination.

Organic and greenhouse gardeners must never take unsterilized soil or compost into their grow area. In addition, potting compost from previous crops must be removed and disposed of in case it contains organisms that are developing immunity to your sprays; especially fungi that will mutate very quickly.

Most problems can be dealt with effectively by using readily available sprays or drenches. A drench is simply poured into the plant container, filling it to the rim, and then allowed to drain away naturally. Organic gardeners who don't want to use chemicals can find a range of safer insecticides that contain natural fatty acids and are particularly good at controlling spider mites. An example is hot pepper wax, which contains a mixture of cayenne peppers and paraffin wax. Pyrethrum is an organic insecticide made from plants and is the grower's main choice for combating infestations. Home-made remedies can also be effective, such as a mild soap solution made with liquid dish detergent that can be sprayed onto the leaves, paying particular attention to the undersides of the plant. Rinse the leaves regularly to ensure the stomata don't become blocked.

Some organic growers plant garlic in with the crop. It takes up very little space and repels most pests. If you want to try this companion planting, buy a variety of garlic that has been bred for cultivation, as it will be disease and virus free. Don't use garlic bulbs from the supermarket.

Flycatchers are sticky strips of brightly coloured plastic card that can be hung around the plants and are very effective at controlling aphids and whiteflies. They are attracted to the card and stick to the surface. Replace the cards once the surface is covered with dead pests.

Whitefly and other pests can be organically controlled using a car vacuum cleaner. Whitefly are best dealt with in the early evening and can be vacuumed from the backs of leaves. Some growers fill the vacuum collection tray or bag with insecticide but it's not essential.

Troubleshooters quick guide / insect and fungal problems

Problem	Indication	Treatment
Algae	*Green slimy growth*	*Clean with H_2O_2. Cover*
Blackfly	*Aphid colonies. Weakens plants*	*Systemic spray. Predators*
Botrytis	*Mould on stems and buds*	*Remove plants. Sprays*
Caspid Bug	*Brown/ red spots. Buds attacked*	*Spray and drench*
Caterpillars	*Irregular holes. Black droppings*	*Remove by hand. Spray*
Damping Off	*Seedlings/ cuttings rot at base*	*Reduce humidity*
Fungi	*White/ dark mould on plants*	*Reduce humidity. Spray*
Greenfly	*Aphid colonies. Twisted growth*	*Systemic spray. Predators*
Mealy bug	*White insects on leaves*	*Spray. Predators*
Sciarid fly	*Black flies. Tiny white maggots*	*Spray/ drench. Predators. Cover pots*
Spidermites	*Tiny clear/ red spiders. Webs*	*Pepper wax/ Pyrethrum/Neem oil/ Predators*
Thrips	*Tiny black or yellow flies*	*Spray. Predators*
Whitefly	*Tiny flies or scales under leaves*	*Spray. Predators*

Troubleshooters quick guide / nutrient disorders

Nutrient	Deficiency	Excess
Calcium	*Plant is stunted. Young leaves turn yellow*	*No direct toxicity*
Copper	*Pale yellow, spotted leaves. Plant is stunted*	*Reduced iron*
Iron	*New growth pales. Yellow between green veins*	*Very uncommon*
Magnesium	*Leaves curled/ brittle. Yellow between veins*	*No direct toxicity*
Molybdenum	*Older leaves turn yellow and leaf margins curl*	*Rare*
Nitrogen	*Leaves chlorotic/ light green. Stunted plant*	*Dark misshapen leaves*
Phosphorous	*Stem/ leaf veins turn yellow/ reddish-purple*	*Copper and zinc reduced*
Potassium	*Chlorosis between green veins, edges burn/ roll*	*Manganese deficiency*
Sulphur	*Young leaves yellow/ purple. Older/ light green*	*Small leaves*
Zinc	*Leaves chlorotic between veins/ necrotic spots*	*Reduced iron*

Smoke bomb treatments are not recommended for grow rooms as they can compromise a setup, but they can be effective in the greenhouse. I met an inmate in prison who was convicted of running what police at that time described as the most sophisticated grow room ever discovered. It had a computer system installed that controlled the growing environment, automatically adjusting CO_2 and measuring and adjusting nutrient levels. The inmate had written the program himself and was a well-educated and intelligent man, with absolutely no common sense. Even his sophisticated system couldn't keep out the humble spider mite, so to rid himself of the problem he ignited two smoke bombs in the middle of his grow room. Anxious neighbours alerted by smoke pouring from the house called the fire brigade, who, on getting no response, broke in to fight the fire. If it were an offence to be an idiot in a public place he'd have been charged with it.

Slugs and snails can cause serious damage to young cannabis plants outdoors, but can be prevented from attacking by smearing petroleum jelly around plant pot rims. If you have planted into the soil, slug pellets are effective at controlling slugs and snails, but they are toxic and harmful to the slug's natural predators such as birds and small mammals. There are non-toxic pellets available and they are worth the extra cost as you are only magnifying the problem if you poison your slug-killing allies. Slug pubs are an excellent and environmentally friendly way of killing slugs and snails. Sink a large plant saucer level with the ground and fill it with beer. Slugs simply can't resist beer and by morning you will find the saucer full of drowned pests.

Predators

Predators are insects that prey on pest species. They are harmless to your crop, and their numbers, once released into the growing area, will be determined by the size of the pest problem. Once the predators have destroyed the pest species, they will die out. In practice, they tend to control the number of pests rather than eradicate them completely. They are, however, effective in continuous yield systems where the grower can't shut the area down. Once you have added your predators, avoid spraying your crop with insecticides. Horticultural suppliers will be able to advise you on the availability of predators. Predators are generally supplied by mail order from specialist breeders. Some growers add ladybirds *Coleoptera coccinellidae,* to their growing environments whenever they can catch them outside as they are natural aphid and spider mite controllers and thrive in greenhouse and grow room conditions, but lamps should be enclosed to prevent them flying into them. A ladybird will consume over 5,000 aphids in its lifetime. There is a tiny wasp called *Aphidius matricariae,* who will also hunt out aphids and inject an egg into the host's back, hunting out small pockets of aphids before they become an infestation. Another good aphid killer is *Aphidoletes aphidimyza*, also known as the *Aphid midge.* This tiny killer is a native of Europe. It mates a few days after hatching and then lays up to 100 eggs near the aphid colony. Within two days the eggs hatch into tiny orange larvae that begin devouring the aphids for up to two weeks before crawling down into the plant medium to develop into a cocoon. The larvae of the European Hoverfly also consume large numbers of aphids. Hoverflies look like wasps but hover around flowers like tiny humming birds. The Hannibal Lector of the predator world is *Chrysopa carnea,* also known as the lacewing. They lay tiny green eggs that hatch in about four days. Lacewing larvae are so aggressive that they will eat each other if they can't find any prey. They viciously attack all soft-bodied pests, including spider mites, and are particularly effective against aphids. They kill even when they don't need to feed, leaving punctured victims to die of their wounds, and they will consume up to 50 aphids per day for three weeks before emerging as adults to repeat the cycle.

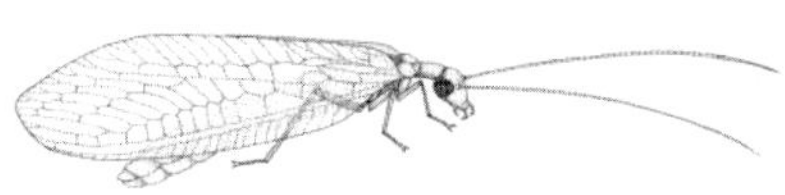

Adult Lacewing (Chrysopa carnea)

If you need a whitefly killer then the *Encarsia formosa* wasp is ideal. It will hunt for the whitefly, which it can detect at up to a metre away, and lay its eggs in the host larvae, killing them. Two weeks later new *E.formosa* appear and the cycle is repeated: they are harmless to humans.

If your plants are suffering from the early stages of a spider mite infestation, you can release a tiny predator mite called *Phytoseiulus persimilus*. They are particularly effective but must be released early to avoid an infestation.

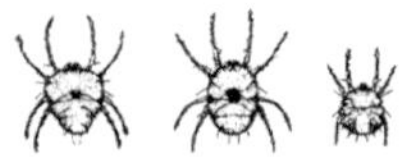
Spider mites (not to scale)

Insect Pests

Spider mites pose by far the greatest threat to cannabis crops and plants exposed to this insect should be treated immediately. If left unchecked, spider mite populations will explode, causing serious damage to the crop and actually killing some plants. The mites appear as either tiny clear or red *arachnids* (spiders). Unlike other mites, they reproduce quickly and several life cycles will be repeated during a growing season. The cycle of egg, nymph, two nymph moults and adult life can take place in under a month. Spider mites don't migrate quickly and move out from the centre of infestation as their population increases. Because they are difficult to spot in the early stages, growers can inadvertently spread the population by taking infested cuttings. Symptoms of attack are the tiny mites themselves moving slowly around the plant, bronzing of the leaves and stems and fine webs on the leaves where mites are active. It will take several treatments to eradicate any infestation; sprays will not kill the eggs. Generally, a once weekly treatment is spread over 5 weeks. Like most arachnids, the spider mite is difficult to treat with regular Diazinon or Dursban treatments, but Pyrethrum is very effective and therefore recommended. Spray the undersides of the leaves to ensure that you kill as many of the mites as possible.

Aphids and other insect pests are less damaging to cannabis, but weaken plants and can transmit viruses, so they should be treated immediately. If you are releasing predators, there are many to choose from, but even truly organic growers should consider using Pyrethrum as a first line of defence. Watch out for earwigs *Dermaptera*, also known as pincer bugs. They feed on aphid eggs, but they also chew cannabis leaves with a passion. Symptoms are irregular holes in the soft parts of the plant's leaves. While not fatal, they can badly damage younger plants. Treat the area with a barrier insecticide powder that you sprinkle around the edge. Greenhouse growers can sometimes mistake baby slug attacks with earwig damage so it is advisable to slug pellet your area as well. Both pests attack at night so by morning you will know the culprit responsible. They should be lying dead on the grow area floor.

Outdoor cultivators can experience problems with roundworms, also known as eelworms. Roundworms are nematodes and there are six species that will attack cannabis plants. They are difficult to diagnose due to their size and because they attack the root system underground. Symptoms to look out for are pockets of plants within the crop showing signs of stunted growth, and problems with wilting during the hotter part of the day, followed by a recovery in the cooler evening. The infestation destroys the root system, starving the plant of water and nutrients. You need to dig down to check the plant's roots. Nematodes that attack cannabis roots cause the formation of root knots or gauls that can easily be seen. They appear as lumps or growths on the roots. Treat the plant with a systemic insecticide and regular root drenches.

The stem nematode, *Ditylenchus dipsaci*, lives above ground and attacks stems, branches and leaf petioles. Symptoms of this infestation are stunted growth with twisted and shortened internodes. Treat with a systemic insecticide.

Parasitic Plants

Parasitic plants are almost exclusively an outdoor problem and can seriously damage cannabis crops. There are two genera of parasitic plants that will attack crops. Broomrape *Orobanche ramosa* is by far the most serious and attacks from under the ground, sinking specialized feeder roots, called haustoria, into the host's own root system to draw away nutrients and fluid. The sites of these haustoria attacks can develop fungal root infections. Broomrapes live entirely under ground and so are impossible to spot. However, they do briefly send up shoots that flower and seed quickly, before dying back. Broomrapes are responsible for huge amounts of damage to hemp fibre crops and will also attack tomato and tobacco plants. Dodder, by contrast, sinks haustoria's into plant tissue above ground and can easily be seen.

Dodder appears as tangles of filaments called Devils ringlets that twine tightly around stems and branches. Left alone, they will eventually pull the host plant over. The European strain of this parasite is known as *Cuscuta europa* and, like broomrape, causes serious damage to French hemp fibre crops.

Fungal Attacks

There are at least 80 species of fungi that will attack cannabis and by far the most serious is *Botrytis cinerea* or Grey mould. Grey mould will attack young seedlings and cause damping off, a symptom of which is brown soft rotting of the vegetable matter at the soil line. The young seedlings quickly topple over and die. The same symptom can occur on cuttings that have been kept in high humidity for too long. Several fungi will cause damping off, including the following:

Rhizoctonia solani
Botrytis cinerea *(can be controlled with carbendazim)*
Macrophomina phaseolina
Fusarium solani
Fusarium oxysporum *(used by the US to destroy drug crops)*
Fusarium sulphureum
Fusarium avenaceum
Fusarium graminearum

Prevalent organisms that are not strictly fungi but belong to the Pythium species also cause damping off, including the following:

Pythium aphanidermatum
Pythium ultimum

Grey mould also attacks the stems of cannabis plants and can be seen as a furry growth around infected areas. The growth becomes covered with fungal spores and the tissue in the infected region becomes soft and rotten. Eventually all growth above the site of attack will die. The other manifestation of grey mould occurs during flowering and attacks the larger resinous buds since, in damp conditions, these buds trap moisture, creating ideal conditions for fungal growth.

The treatment for all fungal infections starts with good prevention. Spray your crop every two weeks with a preventative systemic fungicidal spray, especially during flowering, as it is far easier to prevent attacks than treat them once symptoms appear. Carefully control humidity levels in the growing environment during flowering. Don't allow seedlings and cuttings to get waterlogged and raise all their media out of any standing water, to allow them to drain naturally. Take cuttings out of a humid environment after two days by removing the propagator lid and, although they don't require high light levels, ensure that you have a light source positioned directly above. In greenhouses, try to ensure that the clones receive filtered, indirect sunlight. If your cuttings do suffer from damping off, they can sometimes be rescued by cutting them 2cm above the rot line and dipping the stem into a dilute solution of copper sulphate and ammonium carbonate (Cheshunt compound) before applying fresh rooting gel and placing them into a fresh, well-drained medium.

Stem disease is harder to treat and will kill a lot of plants. They must be removed from the grow area immediately. If you have caught the infection in time you can wipe the affected area very gently with a soft cloth dipped in diluted copper oxychloride and then treat the whole plant with a systemic spray. Repeat this every 10 days until there are no more signs of infection. Keep the plants in a dry environment and drench the medium with a dilute fungal treatment before covering it with foil to prevent evaporation from raising humidity in the treated area. Bud infections are even harder to deal with and the treatment has to be fairly drastic. All infected buds are removed and destroyed. The plant itself must be isolated and placed in a dry environment, in a drenched and covered medium. Treat the plant with a fungicidal spray; however, if it is badly infected it is better to destroy the plant. Prevention of these attacks starts with the early use of systemic fungicidal sprays before any fungi can establish themselves, and by controlling the humidity in your grow area. Clean all surfaces regularly with a 5% dilute bleach solution and remove any dead plant material from the grow area immediately. Outdoor growers should use preventative systemic fungicides as soon as flowering commences, even if there are no symptoms.

Fungal infections can also occur in the leaves of cannabis plants and some can spread into the plant stem, these infections are called leaf spot. Infections are classified by their appearance so identifying the symptoms is made easier.

Yellow and brown leaf spot will not kill cannabis plants but will badly affect the yield. Remove infected plants for spraying with a fungicidal treatment.

Pink leaf spot is a more serious infection caused by *Trichothecium roseum*. This fungal attack will quickly spread and kill your crop if left untreated. Badly infected crops should be destroyed and the grow area disinfected. It is possible to treat pink leaf spot if it is caught early enough; some growers report that copper oxychloride can be effective. Use it as a spray treatment and repeat weekly until the infection has been eradicated.

Viruses

These are spread by parasitic insects, mainly whiteflies, thrips, and aphids. There have been reports of *Hemp mozaic virus* and *Hemp streak virus* being transmitted to European crops by feeding insects and although these are rarely fatal, they will reduce yields. Symptoms of viral infections are chlorosis of the leaves that turn into yellow streaks, or chevron stripes across the surface. Occasionally you will see brown flecks on the leaves. Viruses are impossible to eradicate and the whole of the plant is infected, including seeds and pollen that will carry and spread the infection.

Chemical Treatment Compounds

Bordeaux mixture - *a mixture of copper sulphate and hydrated lime used to control fungal infections*

Cheshunt compound - *a mixture of copper sulphate and ammonium carbonate used to control damping off*

Copper Oxychloride - *controls most fungal infections in cannabis plants*

Sulphur - *used as a treatment for powdery fungal infections*

It is important to remember that your crop is intended for consumption and any chemicals you apply can linger in the plant tissue. Be aware of what you are using and adhere to any applicable withholding periods

Organic Pesticides

Derris - *made from the powdered and dried root of a wild plant but still highly toxic. Its active ingredient is rotenone*

Pyrethrum - *made from the South African Pyrethrum plant. Very safe for the user and kills all pests that attack Cannabis sativa*

Insecticidal soap - *derived from fatty acids of plant origin. Very safe to handle but only kills those insects it is sprayed onto*

Soft soap - *a traditional mixture of plant origin used to control aphids and as a wetting agent*

Neem oil - *effective against spidermites*

Organic gardeners opt for less invasive forms of control, such as hand picking pests, or using insecticidal soap, in order to create a disease and pest free environment that doesn't leave any harmful chemical residue in the crop. Organic growers strive to create a balanced eco system that keeps itself in check

(A) Moroccan 'Soap bar'

Soap bar is made of powdered leaf and a small amount of resin glands or hash oil. PVA-glue, beeswax, paraffin wax and condensed milk are then used to bind the mixture together. Cheap soap has ketamine or other sedatives added to enhance the effect. Henna, or coffee and dark brown shoe polish are then used to colour the mixture before producers add turpentine to disguise the smell and press the nasty mixture into 250g bars for you to smoke! Stick to buds...

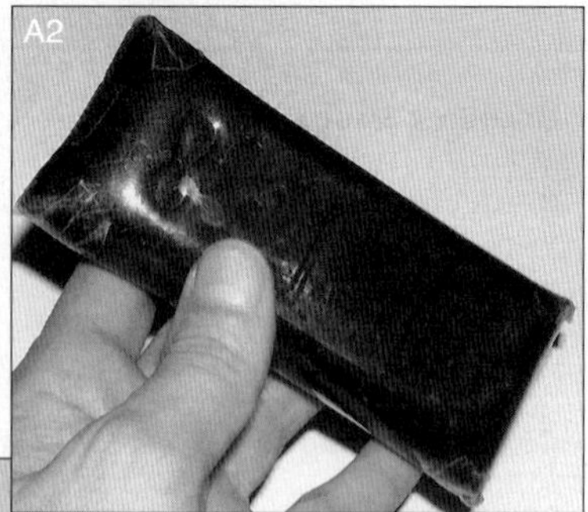

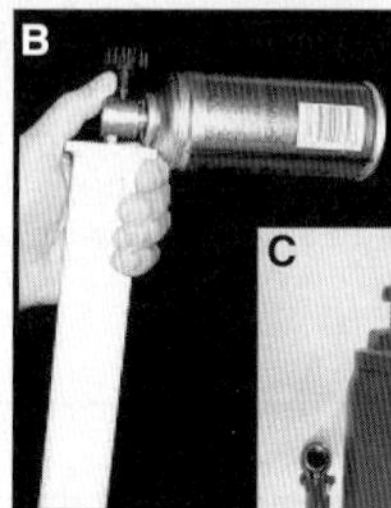

(B) Butane extraction. Very dangerous! Check website for details
(C) Bottle jack used to compress home made hash

(D/E/F) Simple Skuff collection...

Place your dried, crushed trimmings into a pyrex bowl. Lick your finger and rub across one side of the bowl so resin glands stick to the damp surface. Swirl around as if you were panning for gold. Remove the skuff with a dry finger and scrape into storage tube

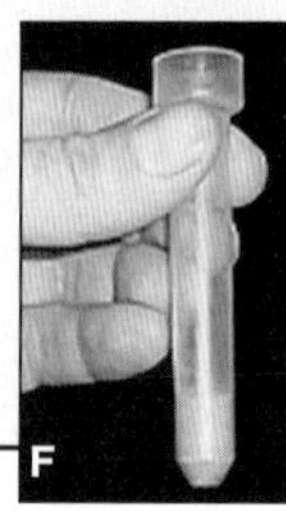

Chapter 15

EXTRACTING THC

Penser, c'est voir. To think is to see. Balzac, 1799–1850

After curing and drying your cannabis crop you will have a collection of manicured and packaged buds ready for consumption. Along with these you will have a large collection of dried leaves, bud trimmings, and possibly male plants. The leaf material contains a low percentage of THC; however, through extraction it can be concentrated into rich, spicy oil that can be smoked or eaten.

There are many different ways to remove the oil from dried cannabis plants. However, in most countries it is difficult to obtain the chemicals that are necessary to complete the extraction. Fortunately, Acetone can be purchased easily within Europe if you know where to look, and it is one of the best chemicals available for home hash oil production. Acetone is a solvent that is used in fibreglass moulding and for cleaning brushes and equipment. Boat builders and auto mechanics all use the chemical, and individuals can purchase it from wholesalers without any questions being asked. Check boating and trade magazines for suppliers. You can also find it in hairdressing and beauty salons where it is used to remove artificial nails. Check out any beauty supply stores in your area, where you can purchase the chemical. If asked, explain that you are a nail technician. If you don't look the part, say it's for someone else.

THC is readily dissolved in acetone and the extractions are more purified than isopropyl alcohol, ethanol or petroleum ethers. The resulting oils have none of the taste associated with some extractants, as very little of the non-psychoactive material is dissolved. Acetone is highly flammable and care needs to be taken since it evaporates rapidly, even at room temperature. Supplies of acetone from a beauty wholesaler will come in plastic bottles, which are fine, but larger amounts purchased for brush cleaning will be in aluminium containers. Store acetone away from any heat sources.

> **Acetone is highly flammable and precautions must be taken**

Acetone (CH3 COCH3)

Acetone is a colourless, flammable, organic solvent also called dimethyl ketone. Prepared by the oxidization of isopropyl alcohol, heating calcium acetate or by the Hock method using benzene as its raw material. It boils at 56°C, which is a very low boiling point, compared to water which boils at 100°C, and alcohol at 78.5°C.

Simple Extraction

1. Take all your dried, cured leaf material and separate it from the plant stalks. Remove any seeds, as they taste bad. Mix smaller buds from the base of the plant in with the leaves and any trimmings from the manicuring process. Extractions made with bud material are two to three times more potent.
2. Super-dry the leaves and flowers to remove all traces of moisture. This is best done in a microwave oven. Place small amounts in at a time and heat for a few minutes. When sufficiently dried, the material should crumble between your fingers.
3. Place the super-dried leaves and flower material into a blender and reduce them to a fine powder. Then pass this powder through a flour sieve and into a large Pyrex bowl.
4. Pour acetone over the powdered plant material in the Pyrex bowl and ensure that it is well covered. Place a sheet of aluminium foil over the bowl to act as a lid and leave the solution for two days at a cool temperature. Store away from any naked flames.
5. After two days take the solution and pour it through a large funnel lined with a filter paper, such as those available in home brewing kits. Alternatively, use a coffee filter or a piece of silk. Collect the liquid and pour it into a container for the final stage.

6. This last stage requires a slow cooker. Slow cookers or crock-pots are readily available from household appliance retailers and are relatively inexpensive to buy. They consist of a ceramic pot and an electric heating unit. Set the slow cooker up outside where the acetone can be safely boiled off into the atmosphere. The fumes given off by this final process are extremely volatile. There must be no naked flames. Cook the acetone solution on the lowest heat setting until all of the solvent has been evaporated. The oil will remain in the bottom of the ceramic container. Once the acetone has evaporated, switch the cooker off, and while it is still warm scrape the oil from the base of the ceramic pot and store it in a glass container. You can get some useful glass containers from a hobby science kit or just use a cup. Acetone evaporates rapidly and it is possible to complete this process outdoors on a sunny day, but it can take days to evaporate a small amount. Don't try and speed up the process using microwaves or heaters. Acetone ignites easily. If you want more malleable oil, leave it suspended in a little solvent, you can then paint this onto cigarette papers and the acetone will evaporate away in seconds.

More Complex Extraction Techniques
The extraction process can be speeded up and made more cost effective by using an apparatus to allow you to heat the acetone solution, and to then collect it by distillation during the final stages. A working knowledge of chemistry is helpful.

The cannabis is prepared in the same way, powdered and covered with acetone, but instead of leaving it to stand for days the solution is heated gently in a specially designed reflux chamber placed in a large water container heated over an electric ring. The temperature of the water is checked with a heat resistant thermometer and kept at 56°C, which is the boiling point of the solvent. The refluxing is continued for three to four hours, depending on the quantities that are being extracted, and then the apparatus is allowed to cool. A condenser is fitted to the apparatus and the solution is heated to 56°C once more. This causes the acetone to vaporise and rise into the distillation section where it can be cooled and collected in a separate vessel.

The extracted oils are removed from the apparatus and stored. Alternatively, the oils can be further purified with laboratory grade filter papers to make Honey Oil, although this will lose you about half of the oil's weight and is only for the connoisseur.

Cannabinoids are the psychoactive compounds found in cannabis plants. Collectively, referred to as THC but they also include CBN and CBD. CBN has been shown to increase the effect that THC has on the user, whereas CBD actually works as a blocking agent. It is possible to convert CBD into THC using a process known as isomerization, but this is best left to the experts. The process entails using sulphuric acid, which is a very aggressive chemical and difficult to obtain. Providing you have used good quality cannabis for your oil, there is no need to worry about CBD.

Making Hashish

THC is contained in multi cellular glandular hairs on the surface of the cannabis plant's leaves and flowers. These hairs are known as stalked capitate trichomes and appear as tiny, translucent mushroom-like structures that can be seen through a magnifying glass. Pure hashish, known as Cream or compressed resin glands (skuff), is made by separating the resin-laden capitate trichomes and compressing them. The quality of your cream will depend on the method used to extract the glands. In its simplest form, the glands may be collected by gently rubbing over the flowering females and then, scraping the resinous deposits off your hands with a knife. The oil will contain some impurities but is composed mainly of trichome heads and stalks. This resin is placed between pieces of plastic wrap and compacted between the palms of your hands. You may already have experienced the sticky resin on your fingers when manicuring your buds.

Most commercially available hash is either silk-screen rubbed, which produces a high quality hash or made from an oil extraction added to a very fine powder made from flower tops. This does not contain the high concentrations of THC that you find in cream, but that does not mean it is of poor quality. Most smokers find that cream is too potent for regular use. Preparing your own powdered flower tops and adding them to the oil you have previously extracted from your crop can make reasonable hashish. The quality of the buds you use to make your powder will reflect on the strength or potency of your hashish. Prepare the flower tops you are going to use by drying them slowly in a cool area to remove as much of the chlorophyll as possible. Some growers soak their buds for a few hours in cold water as this is supposed to extract a certain percentage of chlorophyll, but it is not necessary. Once the flowers are cured, super-dry them in the same way as you would for an oil extraction, except that the final stage is to grind the material to a fine powder using a coffee grinder or mortar and pestle. If you have very resinous buds then this becomes more difficult, but using a pounding action rather than grinding will do the trick. The powder is then simply mixed with your extracted oil. It is better to have the oil slightly diluted with acetone to keep it malleable – the acetone will evaporate slowly at room temperature. Cover your hand with plastic cling film wrap and then knead and roll the mixture into a ball. It is better to use a mould to shape the hash. The mould can be a simple wooden frame that is placed onto foil or plastic wrap and filled with the mixture. Cover the top with more plastic wrap and you can then roll and compress the hash with a rolling pin. You need to apply a lot of pressure while doing this. Many growers prefer to use a bench-mounted vice that can be hand tightened to give good compression to their hash. If you are preparing any quantity of hashish, you may want to construct a heavier press utilizing a car bottle jack.

Mixing equal quantities of powder and oil produces potent hashish. By adding one-part oil to two-parts powder you get a milder, less intense hash similar to Lebanese. By combining the stronger mix with the latex from Papaver somniferum, the opium poppy, you get something similar to Nepalese Temple Ball, although this should always be made with cream.

Cream

Cream, made from compressed resin glands (skuff), is the most potent hashish you can make. There are a variety of methods, other than rubbing the flower tops that a home producer can use. The best cream is made from the buds themselves but any bud trimmings and flower parts can be used. Fan leaves don't have any glands on their surface and are not suitable for use, but smaller leaves from around the flowers can be used. View your plant material through a magnifying glass before deciding if it is suitable. Don't confuse cystolith glands or unicellular hairs for stalked capitate trichomes. If there is no ball structure above the hair it is not a trichome gland. Flowers that are to be used in cream making must be cured in the same way as buds intended for smoking. Even though we do not require any of the plant material itself, cured flower heads make more potent hashish.

Silk Screening

You can purchase screens for this process that are actually made of polyester or saran. They consist of a fine mesh and are used in printing. Most art shops supply the screens. Choose one that has 124 threads per 2.5cm of screen (12XX used in SB4512, SB4514 and SB4699 Kits). The tighter the mesh the greater the potency; however, there is a corresponding drop in volume produced. Alternatively, you can make a screen by stretching a fine silk stocking over a frame, but this is not very effective. The screen needs to be supported approximately 3cm above a mirror or sheet of aluminium foil that acts as your collection plate for the trichome glands. The flowers are broken gently onto the surface of the screen and moved around the mesh using a plastic phone card. The more pressure you apply to the bud material, the more plant matter will fall through onto the foil. This will make a difference to the potency of the hash and it becomes harder to compress. You will not extract all of the trichomes with flat screening so the buds you have used can still be smoked, although they are not as potent. Once you have collected the glands on the foil, remove your screen and using a phone card, scrape the deposits together to remove the newly formed cream. Compress it between your hands in plastic wrap. It is a very potent smoke and certainly unlike any commercial hashish. If you need to store it, keep it in a cool place in a lightproof container to preserve it. A refrigerator is fine but don't freeze your cream as this can affect its potency.

Shakers

These work by holding your flower tops in a small plastic container with a fine internal mesh. By shaking the container, the trichome glands are dislodged and collected. Shakers are not particularly efficient but will produce a reasonable amount of skuff. Shakers can be purchased from specialist suppliers and are relatively inexpensive. You also can collect resin glands using a specially made storage container. It requires a silkscreen base for your buds to sit on and a removable collection box located underneath. As you handle and prepare your buds the resin glands fall through the silkscreen and are collected in the shallow container underneath.

Food Processors

Resin glands, when placed into water, sink, whereas plant material that has been chopped and dried will float. In order to ensure that the glands are not too sticky to separate, this process is best carried out using very cold water. Fill your processor half way with buds or trimmings and then add all of the ice from an ice cube tray. Top the remainder up with cold water and blend for two to three minutes. You should end up with a green, ice water mix that you then pour through a large funnel into a clear glass or plastic jug. Line the funnel with a filter made from a silkscreen with 124 threads per 2.5cm of screen. This allows the glands to pass through, but traps the larger plant matter. You now need to remove the glands from the water, which is best done with a coffee filter or a piece of silk. The water will pass through, leaving the skuff in the filter. The skuff is then dried and compressed as before. It is not the purest of cream but it is certainly very potent.

Tumblers

Tumblers are mechanical separators that consist of a revolving drum and silk-screen rim. The dried flowers are gently agitated as the drum slowly spins, allowing the glands to fall through the silkscreen to be collected at the base of the drum on foil. The secret lies in their slow rotation and they produce the purest cream you can make with no plant material contaminants. These machines are on sale in the Netherlands, but they are also cheap and easy to build yourself using the motor from a barbecue rotisserie to turn your drum. The drum itself is constructed from MDF (multi-density fibre board), available at most building supply stores. The MDF should not be more than 10mm thick. You need to cut two 400mm circles from the board. Mark the circle with a piece of string pinned to the centre, with your pencil tied to the end of it. It is best to use a jigsaw to cut the shape, and then round it off smooth with a file and sandpaper.

You now need a length of threaded bar that has a slightly larger diameter than the rotisserie spit shaft opening. This size can vary but is not a problem as you simply file the end of the bar square to fit the opening. Then drill the centres of the two MDF discs you have cut the same diameter as the threaded bar. Mount the unit onto a small bench made from MDF board that has been cut into a 60cm square. Then cut out a 50 x 20cm section from the middle. This is where the wheel will rotate, with the rotisserie motor fixed to one side of the opening and a support mounted on the opposite side to hold the threaded axle. Mount the bench on sturdy legs that give the rotating drum clearance and allow you to catch the glands on foil below. The legs can be made from short sections of 10 x 5cm timber. You will need to brace these with struts to keep them stable. Take one of the MDF discs and mark out an access panel close to the rim at least 15 x 15cm. Cut this out with a jigsaw. This is how you will place and remove your flower tops from the finished drum. The opening is simply covered with a piece of acetate, or stiff plastic held on with duct tape. The buds are stripped of glands by the tumbling process and are usually discarded after use. The drum can be cleaned with a vacuum hose.

You now assemble the drum by passing the axle through the centre holes in your discs. Hold the sides of the discs in position with nuts and large washers threaded onto the shaft and bolted either side. Leave a gap of 15cm between the discs and fix 4 x 2cm wooden dowels around the inside edge to support the wheel structure and assist in the tumbling process by agitating the flowers as they rotate. The silk-screen mesh can now be stretched around the rims and held in position using a hot glue gun and tacks. Glue any joins you make in the mesh with the glue gun. Place your newly assembled drum into the bench opening and then mount the rotisserie motor to one side attaching it to the axle shaft. The size and position of motors varies and you will need to do some fine-tuning at this stage to ensure that the axle, motor and opposite axle mounting are level and secure. Support the axle on the opposite side of the motor on a short piece of 10 x 5cm timber with a groove cut into the top to sit the axle in. You can line this with a section of copper water pipe cut in half and glue gunned into position. Ensure that your bench legs give you ample clearance, position your foil, and your machine is ready to go. Fill the drum with flower tops and trimmings and then leave it to slowly rotate. The buds fall to the bottom of the drum as they are slowly tumbled. After 30 minutes you will have collected your first skuff on the foil. Collect and compress it: it is the purest cream you can get. You now need to place a small rubber ball into the drum with your flower tops and then switch the machine back on again for at least an hour. The ball helps to agitate the buds. This process produces a lower grade of skuff, but it is still exceptional. Once you have mastered this technique you can experiment with different size meshes to build your perfect cream maker.

Nepalese Temple Ball

Temple ball is prepared from a mixture of cream and the dried latex from the opium poppy. It is not illegal to cultivate poppies in most of Europe but the harvesting and possession of opium latex is against the law. The opium poppy's botanical name is Papaver somniferum, meaning sleep inducing. The history of this plant is unclear; some horticulturists believe it evolved naturally while others think it is a cultivar developed by man. Either way it is most likely to have evolved from *Papaver setigerum,* the wild poppy that does contain small amounts of opium. There is another close relative of *Papaver somniferum* that also produces significant opium quantities, which is known by its botanical name *Papaver bracteatum.*

Papaver somniferum is an annual with a growth cycle of around 120 days. It is similar to cannabis in that it is photo-responsive and requires 12-hour light cycles to produce flowers. It can be successfully cultivated under HPS lamps indoors and thrives in hydroponic systems. Its nutrient requirements are similar to cannabis but it prefers an acidic medium. Organic crops of poppies should be started indoors. The seeds are tiny but generate quickly in a warm, moist environment. Use peat pots for germination, since poppies are notoriously difficult to transplant; they cannot tolerate any root damage. Peat pots degrade naturally once in the soil, allowing the delicate roots to grow through. Poppies are sown in early spring and need a sunny location with well-drained soil. The plant will reach a height of 90 to 150cm and flower in the autumn or in a 12-hour light cycle. Unlike cannabis, poppies are not dioecious. The buds all produce four large petals, with dark spots at the base that vary in colour from white through to purple. The main stem and each tiller, end in a single flower bud. As these flower buds develop, the ends of the penduncle and tillers extend and bend towards the ground, forming a distinctive hook shape.

The main alkaloids in opium latex are:

Morphine
Noscapene
Papaverine
Codeine

The alkaloids are a highly complex organic base of nitrogen, water and acids.

The young buds form upside down. As the bud matures the stems straighten upwards and within two days of becoming vertical the bud sepals open and the flower blooms. The flowers only last four days before the petals drop to expose a small round pod. This is the seedpod that will grow ovular in shape and narrow at the top as the seeds ripen and are eventually released through small holes in the crown. When mature, the pod will measure between 5 and 8cm in diameter. Two weeks after the petals drop you can harvest the latex.

The pod is cut with three sets of three incisions from the crown to the base of the pod. It is important that the cuts are of the correct depth. Incisions that are too deep will cause internal weeping of the latex that will kill the seed head. If the incisions are too shallow the pod will heal and latex will not flow out. The correct depth is (1.25mm) with a tolerance of (0.25mm). The traditional tool for harvesting opium is a three-blade instrument that allows you to cut each set in one action. You can use a craft knife to carry out this process but ensure it has a retractable blade that can be set to the correct depth.

The latex weeps from the cuts and first appears as a white malleable substance that oxidizes on contact with air and turns into a brown viscous gum. Scrape the brown gum off with a wet blade and dry it in the sun for several days until it takes on the consistency of soft wax and becomes raw opium. Once dried, the raw opium is stable. Over time, the opium slowly loses moisture and become more concentrated. You can expect to yield 70mg per pod.

Raw opium typically contains about 7% plant material contaminants that are undesirable for smoking. A process known as cooking removes these contaminants. Dissolve the opium in boiling water then pass the water-opium solution through a fine filter to remove the plant material. Bring the liquid opium solution back to the boil, and evaporate the water off, leaving a brown paste known as smoking opium. Allow this paste to slowly dry and harden. Then, powder the opium in a mortar and pestle or coffee grinder and add it to freshly collected, unpressed resin glands (cream). Compress this mixture between cling film using your hands. Temple ball is traditionally hand-rolled into small round balls.

Add 1-gram of opium to 7-grams of cream.

I have added this section because I feel it is relevant. It is up to you how you choose to use it but you must be aware that opium is an insidious, seductive and dangerous substance that causes dependence. It is not without reason that opium and its derivatives are known as 'Nasty' in London slang.

There are many ways to use cannabis without smoking tobacco...

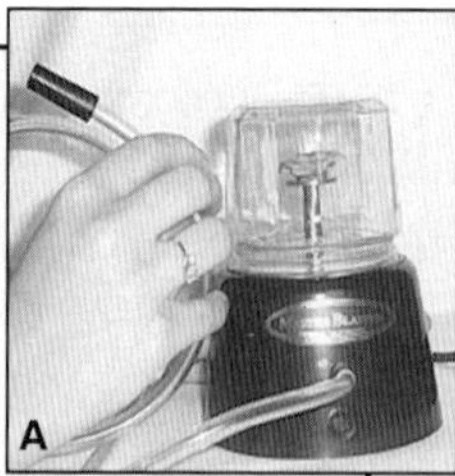

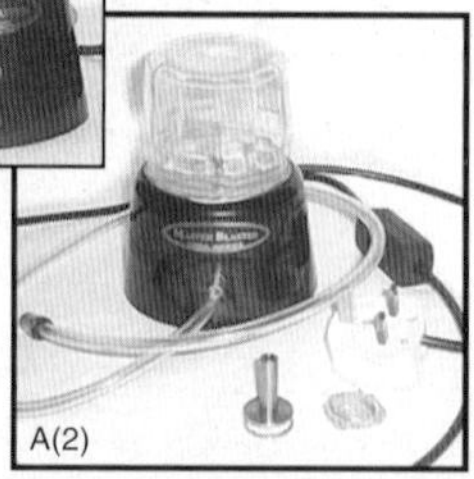

Vaporiser

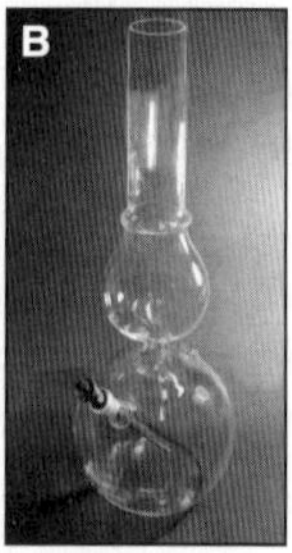

Water cooled bong

(A) Vaporiser
(B) Water bong
(C) Cured bud
(D) Cannabis pipe
(E) THC dissolves readily in milk;
(F) and butter;
(G) for use in hash cakes / milk drinks.
(H) Cannabis tincture

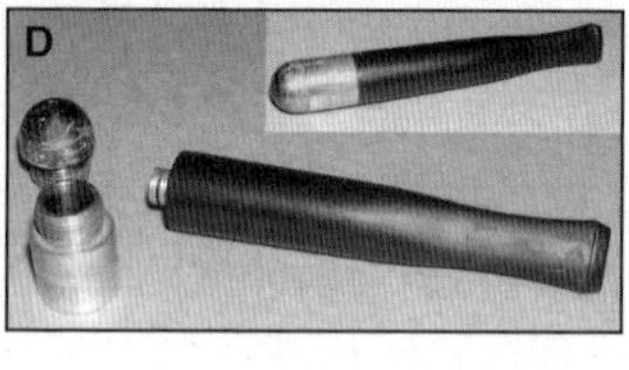

Chapter 16

ENJOY!

One half of the world cannot understand the pleasures of the other. Jane Austin

Cannabis bud, weed, resin and oil is generally smoked in hand rolled cigarettes, either mixed with tobacco, herbs, or on its own known as *Iytal.* It can also be smoked in small pipes called chillums or in larger water-cooled Bongs. Others prefer to heat cannabis on a hot knife and inhale the vapours through a tube. In 500 BC the Greek writer Heroditus described the use of cannabis by the Scythians who made sweat tents where cannabis seeds (and it is assumed flowers) were thrown onto burning embers and the fumes inhaled. This would have released large amounts of THC into the confined area and it is hardly surprising that Heroditus claimed users, 'howled with pleasure'. Cannabis can be used to make drinks such as *Bhang lassi,* while others make Tinctures of cannabis by dissolving it in strong spirits. Tinctures can be used recreationally, and in herbal remedies to alleviate most of the illnesses described later, many patients mix cannabis tincture with herbal teas such as camomile, or rosehip or alternatively it can be made into linctus for treating chest and breathing problems. In many countries it is traditional to cook with cannabis and it is added to a variety of dishes, this is a pleasant way to enjoy your cannabis but always remember that ingested cannabis is stronger and slightly hallucinogenic so only use small amounts.

Smoking Cannabis

Hand rolled cigarettes or *Joints* are usually made by joining two cigarette papers. The best way to do this is to overlap two *skins* slightly, and moisten the gum on the edge that is touching, then take a third paper and fold it in half with the gum outermost. Moisten the glue on both sides and then place it between the first two sheets and press them together, then slide out the folded paper and the gum will remain to secure your king size papers. Others prefer to join three papers together with one stuck to the bottom and the third turned and gummed along the edge. The joint is then rolled in a slight cone shape that is fatter at the lit end, and a small tube of card is placed in the end to act as a *roach*. It is better to leave out the roach and place the filter from a cigarette in the end to reduce the damage tobacco tars can do to your lungs.

The *Tulip* is a connoisseur's joint that is difficult to roll but consists of three papers joined to form a square. The cannabis and tobacco are mixed and rolled into a short fat cone in the papers and they are twisted at the end. A thin tube is then rolled from card and secured with cigarette papers and this is inserted into the opposite end of the bulb shaped cone, and secured. The finished joint looks like a Dutch tulip flower. Pipes and chillums are available made specifically for smoking cannabis and these are worth investing in, alternatively tobacco pipes can be used. Small clay and cob pipes are excellent for smoking weed. There are a variety of specialized pipes available including one that resembles a credit card that can be discreetly carried. There are other designs available that incorporate small hash pipes in belt buckles and ballpoint pens and these are ideal if you are away from home. But if you intend to travel abroad leave them behind. Customs officers actively look for drug paraphernalia.

Bongs can be homemade from plastic bottles with a bowl and tube secured at the top. The bowl can be made from a socket set attachment with the plastic tube wedged into its base. Kitchen foil lines the inside of the socket attachment and is repeatedly perforated with a pin. Half fill the bottle with water and then fix the bowl in place with heat-proofed mastic, ensuring the pipe reaches into the water. Next make a small hole above the waterline and fix your smoking tube to it, ensure it is airtight with some clear mastic or *Blue tack* and you are ready to enjoy your water-cooled cannabis.

Cannabis fumes can be smoked in a Vaporiser that gives a cool and smooth taste that many smokers at first find strange. A large percentage of THC is destroyed in the burning process used to create the smoke in pipes and joints. Activation of THC acids called *decarboxylation* occurs at around 103 °C with vapourisation taking place at around 200 °C. Vaporisers gently heat the cannabis to a temperature where the cannabinoids evaporate. This is below the temperature that plant material will burn at, but still allows the vapours to be collected and inhaled. Vaporisers can be purchased from specialist suppliers and are a healthy way to enjoy cannabis, especially for medicinal users. Oil can be smoked in joints or chased off kitchen foil. A small amount is smeared onto the foil and then heated from underneath with a lighter, the resulting fumes are inhaled through a cardboard tube. Joints can be fitted into a hole made in the of the base of a cardboard tube. The end of the tube is covered with the smoker's hand and the fumes are inhaled through the opposite opening. To increase the 'hit' the smoker removes his hand and finds out why this method of smoking is called a Shotgun.

Those smokers who have yet to try a Bottle and bucket or Gravity bong are missing a cannabis smoking experience. A plastic bottle has the base cut away and a foil lid is pushed into the neck and perforated with a pin. The bottle is then gently pushed into a bucket of water then hash, weed or oil is placed into the foil bowl and lit. The bottle is then drawn slowly upwards and the resulting vacuum sucks the smoke into the bottle. When the bottle is full of rich, pungent cannabis smoke the foil bowl is removed and the smoker places their mouth over the bottle opening and then pushes the bottle back down into the water. This forces the smoke straight out of the bottle to be enjoyed by the rapidly stoned citizen.

Cannabis Tincture

THC can be dissolved into fats, milk, oil and alcohol but not water so one way to enjoy a cannabis drink is to add it to your favourite spirit. Dry and powder your weed then place it into a container with an airtight lid. Soak it overnight in water to remove any impurities then drain and replace the water with spirit. Leave the mixture for at least a week before straining the liquid through a funnel lined with filter paper and pouring the mixture back into the spirit bottle. Most connoisseurs of cannabis tincture prefer to add it to brandy, fruit Schnapps or liqueurs as the cannabis can have a bitter taste.

Cooking with Cannabis

Cannabis cooking is based on the principle that THC needs to be dissolved into either fat or oil. Once you have done this you can then use the extraction in your recipes. The most favoured fat to use is butter or *Ghee* and the usual ratio for Hash butter is:

50-grams powdered flowers / hash + 500-grams of butter

Heat the butter gently to soften it, and then stir in your powder. It will take 20 to 30 minutes for the cannabis to dissolve into the butter so allow it to gently heat through, and stir occasionally. Cannabis oil or hash does not require as long. If you don't want any flower particles in the butter you can pass it through a sieve, muslin cloth or stocking. Alternatively smaller amounts can be dissolved into vegetable oil heated in a teaspoon over a flame. This is useful for making potent Hash yoghurt. Allow the oil to cool before mixing it into the yoghurt pot. Non alcoholic drinks can be made by simmering cannabis in milk for 30 minutes, before straining. If you wish to add the milk to tea or coffee it needs to be fairly strong. It's a common misconception that tea can be made by pouring boiling water over cannabis flowers. THC does not dissolve in water.

Recipes you may wish to try

Breakfast Buds. *A healthy start to the day.*

Sprinkle two teaspoons of dried and powdered cannabis flowers onto one bowl of breakfast cereal.

Add milk with yoghurt, fruit, sugar or honey to taste.
Enjoy.

Harrera. *Traditional Moroccan soup served at the end of Ramadan.*

Finely chop, 1 onion, 1 celery stick, 1 parsnip and a small bunch of parsley. Cover the bottom of a large saucepan with half a centimetre of olive oil and place on a medium heat. Into this sprinkle two heaped tablespoons of pulverized hash or weed and stir for 10 minutes, before adding the vegetables. Cook the vegetables in the oil then add 1 litre of water, half a cup of peas and 25-grams of fine noodles. Add paprika, salt and pepper to taste and allow it to simmer for 15 minutes. Remove from the heat and add two beaten eggs.
Serve at once with sliced lemon.

Majoon. *An Islamic delicacy.*

Powder 1 cup of buds and add:
Half a cup of chopped almonds, the same of dates, and figs. 1 tablespoon of honey, and a teaspoon of ginger, then nutmeg and finally cinnamon. Dissolve the cannabis into a small amount of butter. Place all the ingredients into a saucepan of water and simmer for 10 minutes stirring occasionally as it reduces.
Turn off the heat and allow to cool slightly before adding a dash of orange juice, then stir the mixture again before pouring it into a shallow baking tray to set.

Cut the sweetmeat into cubes and serve.

Polm Chocolade Taart. *A Dutch treat.*

Melt 250-grams of butter over a low heat and add 25-grams of powdered polm or you can use weed, stir gently for 20 minutes then pass it through a sieve to remove any plant material, reheat and add 200-grams of cooking chocolate and dissolve it into the butter. Next gradually add 250-grams of sugar and mix well before adding four beaten eggs and 200-grams of flour; once again mix well in.
When the mixture is smooth add a further 100-grams of dark Dutch or Belgium chocolate and dissolve. Finally pour the mixture into a shallow baking tray and place in a moderate oven for 30 minutes, allow to cool then slice and serve.

A

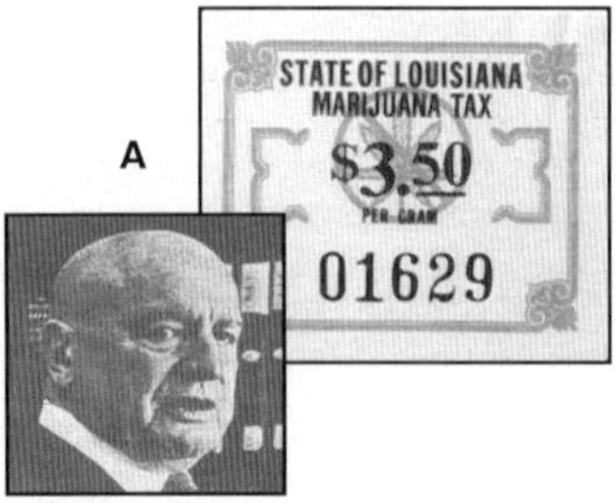

(A) US Marijuana tax stamp and the now discredited Harry J. Anslinger
(B) Pulp fiction
(C) Cannabis has been available in Europe for hundreds of years

B

UK Class C Reclassification (1/07/03)
Under UK law cannabis is now reclassified as a class 'C' controlled substance. This does not mean it is legal, cultivators and dealers will still be prosecuted

Chapter 17

PROHIBITION

To see what is right and not to do it is want of courage. Confucius

Cannabis is by far the most widely used illegal drug in the world. Several million people have tried it at least once: even former US president Bill Clinton admitted to trying cannabis once or twice while studying in England, but claimed he didn't like it and did not inhale. Cannabis use causes no lasting physical or psychological damage and there is no evidence to suggest that it leads to experimentation with other drugs. It does not produce physical dependence, although regular users can develop a psychological need for the drug's calming effect. However, there is some recent evidence of mild physical dependence in 'frequent chronic users'.

Cannabis cultivation for fibre and seed predates written history however many theories surround its early psychedelic use, including the role psycho-active plants may have played in the evolution of consciousness by introducing to us some concept of a spiritual dimension and perhaps the notion of religion. The Shaman was pivotal in early society, however, shamanism is not a religion, but a set of techniques, the principle being that the use of psychedelic plants, which are taken to dissolve boundaries, allow the shaman to step outside and beyond the confines of learned culture and invented language and into the domain of the ideas, a state of consciousness referred to as 'The unspeakable' by Lichtenstein. Around 1000 years before the birth of Christ, cannabis was mentioned in the Hindu sacred text Atharvaveda *(science of charms)* as Sacred Grass, one of the five sacred plants of India and cannabis is still used in ritual offerings to Shiva today. Interestingly, most orthodox religions stem from regions where cannabis was traditionally consumed and Aleister Crowley, author of The Psychology of Hashish written in 1908, argued that perhaps only those momentarily freed from the boundaries of convention by hashish could obtain this spiritual knowledge and furthermore could not do so by any other means. Probably the most relevant study to date on typical cannabis experience concluded; 'Cannabis gives spontaneous insights into self', implying that cannabis use can become a gateway for thoughts and perceptions that are outside conventional understanding. These are not just confined to so-called spiritual experiences and to a certain extent users control what they want to perceive, many are content to use cannabis as a sedative narcotic while others harness the drug more creatively. Cannabis was readily available in 16th and 17th century Europe, Shakespeare wrote of *Invention in a noted weed (sonnet 76)*. His sonnets are full of riddles but include references to the effect of substances distilled from flowers,

...But flowers are distilled, though they with winter meet, leese but their show; their substance still lives sweet' (Sonnet 5)...

Traces of cannabis have been discovered in Elizabethan clay pipes and there is a high probability that William Shakespeare had experience of cannabis use. Cannabis occurs frequently in ancient Semitic languages and appears several times throughout the Old Testament as *kaneh bosm*, which in traditional Hebrew is *kannabos* or *kannabus. Kan* meaning reed of hemp and *bosm* meaning aromatic;

...Moreover the Lord spoke unto Moses, saying, "Take thou also unto thee principal spices, of pure myrrh five hundred shekels, and of cinnamon half so much, even two hundred and fifty shekels, and of sweet Kaneh bosm two hundred and fifty shekels". (Exodus chapter 30)...

The Sythians had introduced hemp into Northern Europe by 500 BC however records also show Marco Polo introduced seeds in 1297 and Christian Crusaders returned with hemp seeds from the Middle East. Traditional folk remedies list cannabis as a tonic, antispasmodic, analgesic, sedative and anodyne, seeds were given to teething infants and preparations of the plant were used to treat conditions ranging from snake bites to Gonorrhoea. The 11th century Anglo-Saxon

Herbarium specifically recommends *haenep* in the treatment of breast pain and by 1588 Tudor herbalists in England grew 85% of their own drug plants, listing *water of hempe* as a treatment for fevers in 'The Vertuous Boke of Distillacioun' *(Andrewes).*

Cannabis is thought to have been introduced into South America in 1545 by the Spanish and some believe the Mexican word marijuana is of Christian origin, Maria *(Mary)* and Juan *(John)* being the names of Jesus' mother and disciple. Although the British had introduced hemp to the newly established Jacobean colonies of Virginia by 1611, they called male cannabis plants *Carl* and females *Fimble* hemp, the word 'marijuana' was adopted by Americans in the 1900's when they were introduced to new drug varieties by migrating Mexican labourers in the South West.

The El Paso city council calculated that cannabis prohibition would be a convenient way of controlling the unpopular Mexicans and in 1914 passed the El Paso Ordinance Act of 1914, banning cannabis in the state. The new Marijuana laws gave police added powers to arrest and harass migrant workers and to this day arrests for cannabis offences are more likely to occur on non-white racial groups.

Cannabis was also arriving in American port cities, transported by West Indian sailors. Cannabis had been introduced into Jamaica by Asian Indian workers migrating to farm the sugar plantations after the abolition of Slavery and Jamaicans still use the Indian name for cannabis, *Ganja.* In New Orleans it became known as *muggles, tea* or *reefer* in the popular jazz clubs where it was consumed, however, its use was once again associated with an unpopular ethnic minority and became a focal point for racist politicians.

Its migration North was inevitable and prompted formation of the Federal Narcotics Bureau headed by the right wing, evangelical extremist, Harry J. Anslinger who began an orchestrated campaign of propaganda and misinformation regarding cannabis use and its effects. The newspapers ran sensational headlines with graphic accounts of violent crime, madness and murder caused by *reefer* use, Anslinger himself gave press and radio interviews;

...Parents beware! Your children, homeward bound from school, are being introduced to a new danger in the form of the drug cigarette, 'marijuana'. A Chicago woman, watching her daughter die as an indirect result of smoking marijuana told officers at least fifty of the girls young friends were slaves to this narcotic...

The American film industry, slow to respond to Anslinger's repeated requests for cooperation were targeted and several high profile arrests followed, including that of Robert Mitchum who was charged with cannabis possession. The industry swiftly complied with Anslinger's wishes giving him full editorial control over all movies containing any reference to narcotics and as a direct result of his intervention many feature films were simply banned. Anslinger's tireless campaign against cannabis use continued unabated and on June 14th 1937 the Marijuana Tax Act was passed in the United States, effectively making cannabis illegal. Anslinger's behaviour was both bizarre and sinister, when scientists began to dispute his claims regarding the effects of cannabis use and presented him with the evidence from various trials he destroyed the documents and discredited the experts. By 1961 Anslinger had gained sufficient power and influence to insist the United Nations follow American drug policies and 100 member states were coerced into signing an agreement virtually outlawing cannabis worldwide. It remains illegal in most countries to this day; however, prohibition has little to do with any concerns for the cannabis users health. Contradicting Anslinger, a United Kingdom House of Lords committee concluded;

...The acute toxicity of cannabis and the cannabinoids is very low: no one has ever died as a direct and immediate consequence of medical or recreational use...

If Anslinger truly believed what he was saying about 'marijuana' then he was an idiot, if not he was a liar; however, his extremist policies remain in force throughout most of Europe to this day.

Many studies have been used to justify the prohibition argument but they have all been discredited, including the most notable among them that suggested that cannabis use caused brain damage. The tests that were used to 'prove' this were unscientific and unethical. Rhesus monkeys were forced to smoke cannabis vapours through a face mask for five minutes at a time, without any supplementary oxygen. The resulting brain tissue damage, which the scientists tried to say was caused by cannabis smoke, was in fact caused by oxygen starvation.

There have been other studies reporting that cannabis smoke is carcinogenic and twice as harmful as tobacco. These studies have also been disproved. All smoke inhaled into the lungs will cause irritation; however, unlike tobacco, cannabis smoke does not attack the bronchiole airways and any irritation to the larger air passages disappears when cannabis use is discontinued.

Tobacco smoke is killing more people each year than class 'A' drugs, AIDS and murder combined. It is more addictive than heroin, with users suffering withdrawal symptoms and relapses similar to those of heavy drug users. One in seven deaths is attributed to tobacco use and the industry needs over one thousand new smokers a day to replace its casualties. Tobacco is legal and subject to taxation by our respective governments.

The absurdity of the prohibition of cannabis is best demonstrated in the Netherlands. Although possession of cannabis for personal use is permitted and it is possible to purchase small amounts from licensed coffee shops, in one 12-month period, 41,884 kilos of hashish were seized by the Amsterdam police and destroyed. Dutch law as it stands both encourages the smuggling of cannabis to supply the coffee shops and wastes police resources in attempting to stop it. Despite decriminalisation it is estimated that there are only between 220,000 and 400,000 regular cannabis users in Holland. In the United Kingdom, Netherlands, France and Germany, cannabis accounts for over 90% of all illegal drug use. This trend is echoed throughout Europe and North America, although the percentage of the population that has at some point tried any drug at least once diminishes.

In most European states, the police no longer prosecute citizens for possession of small amounts of cannabis. To possess an insignificant quantity of cannabis is not illegal in Germany but the federal states still cannot agree on what an insignificant quantity is. Personal use of cannabis in Italy, Spain and Portugal has effectively been decriminalised but cultivation and distribution are still treated as serious offences.

In the United Kingdom cannabis has been reclassified as a class C drug (effective from 1/07/03) and those caught in possession of personal amounts will ordinarily be cautioned for the offence. However, this does not mean that cannabis is legal in the UK, cultivation and supply are still vigorously prosecuted.

Our Swiss neighbours have a more relaxed attitude towards cannabis cultivation and use, plant nurseries there actually grow cannabis crops, although this is not due to legalization of the drug. There exists a loophole in Swiss law that allows dried cannabis to be used as a potpourri to scent your home and full legalization in Switzerland is not far away. In the meantime cultivators play a cat and mouse game with the authorities, with one farmer having his fields surrounded by police officers who supervised the crops conversion into perfume, despite the fact that Switzerland is a neutral country and didn't ratify the UN treaty. Prisons worldwide are full of people serving sentences for cannabis-related offences. The resources spent by our respective governments for cannabis policing policies are huge and ultimately it is taxpayers that fund them. This ancient plant has benefited mankind throughout history yet the campaign to legalize its use is still met with furious opposition from politicians and law enforcement agencies alike. The same ignorance and prejudice is repeated time and again. On my last prison sentence for producing cannabis, I was made to complete three separate courses designed to address my offending behaviour, as I refused to accept that there were any victims in my case. The prison officials continually blocked my attempts to be moved to a lower security prison until I had completed the courses. I heard the same flawed arguments over and over again, from people who I am sure were well intentioned, but just stupid. I still maintain that the only victims of my cannabis production were the skunk connoisseurs of London, who lost one of their best suppliers.

There are thousands of medical cannabis users throughout the world who have found that cannabis relieves disorders ranging from asthma to cancerous tumours. It is unreasonable that people are denied relief because of repressive legislation and that people are still being jailed for growing cannabis plants in the 21st century.

Potted History

2700 B.C. First instance of cannabis use is recorded.
1500 B.C. Scythians cultivate cannabis and use it to weave fine hemp cloth.
1200 - 800 B.C. Cannabis is mentioned in the Hindu sacred text Atharvaveda.
700 - 300 B.C. Scythian tribes leave Cannabis seeds as offerings.
500 B.C. Hemp is introduced into Northern Europe by the Scythians.
500 - 100 B.C. Hemp spreads throughout northern Europe. 430 B.C. Herodotus reports on use of Cannabis.
100 B.C. - 0 Cannabis is mentioned in the herbal Pen Ts'ao Ching.
400 A.D. Cannabis is cultivated in England for the first time in East Anglia at a place called Old Buckenham Mere.
500 - 600 A.D. The Jewish Talmud mentions Cannabis.
1231. Hashish introduced to Iraq.
1271 - 1295. Journeys of Marco Polo in which he reports using hashish.
1378. Turkish Ottoman Emir Soudoun Scheikhouni issues first edict against hashish.
1494. Hemp paper making begins in England.
1563. Queen Elizabeth I, passes a law requiring all landowners with over 60 acres to grow cannabis crops or face a £5 fine.
1776. United States declaration of independence is drafted on cannabis paper.
1798. Napoleon declares a total prohibition among soldiers returning to France.
1842. Queen Victoria's personal physician prescribes cannabis for her menstrual cramps claiming it to be, 'one of the most valuable medicines we possess'.
1843. Le Club des Hachichins, or Hashish Eater's Club, established in Paris.
1850 Hashish appears in Greece.
1856 British tax ganja and charas trade in India.
1875. Cultivation for hashish introduced to Greece.
1877 Kerr reports on Indian ganja and charas trade.
1884. The British Raj in India conduct one of the first studies into cannabis use and conclude it is harmless and helpful.
1893. 1894 70,000 to 80,000 kg of hashish legally imported into India from Central Asia each year.
1901. A Royal commission concludes that cannabis is relatively harmless and not worth prohibiting
1912. Cannabis control is raised at the first International Opium Conference.
1915. Cannabis begins to be prohibited for non-medical use in the US. In; California (1915), Texas (1919), Louisiana (1924), and New York (1927).
1928. Cannabis is made illegal in Britain following the passing of the dangerous drugs act 1925.

MAPS/NORML Study Shows Vaporizers Reduce Toxins in Marijuana Smoke
By Dale Gieringer, Ph.D.
NORML California State Coordinator

MAPS Bulletin. Volume XI, Number 2.

Medical marijuana patients may be able to protect themselves from harmful toxins in marijuana smoke by inhaling their medicine using an electric vaporizer, according to initial results of a study by the Multi-disciplinary Association for Psychedelic Studies (MAPS) and California NORML. Research expenditures to date are roughly $50,000.

The study showed that it is possible to vaporize medically active tetrahydrocannabinol (THC) by heating marijuana to a temperature short of the point of combustion, thereby eliminating or substantially reducing potentially harmful smoke toxins that are normally present in marijuana smoke. Vaporizers may therefore substantially reduce what is widely regarded as the leading health concern associated with marijuana, namely respiratory harm due to smoking. In addition, many medical marijuana patients say they prefer vaporizers because they deliver smoother, less irritating medication.

MAPS and NORML sponsored the study in the hopes of helping medical marijuana patients and others reduce the health risks of smoking marijuana. A major obstacle to approval of natural cannabis by the Institute of Medicine (IOM) in its 1999 report, "Marijuana and Medicine," was that smoking is an "unhealthy" delivery method. The IOM report failed to note the possibility of vaporization. The MAPS-NORML study tested a device called the M1 Volatizer(R), an aromatherapy vaporizer developed by Alternative Delivery Systems, Inc. It consisted of an electric heating element in a chamber that radiates heat downwards over a sample of marijuana contained in a standard bowl. Output from the vaporizer was analysed and compared to smoke produced by burning the sample.

The vaporizer produced THC at a temperature of 200° C. (392° F.) while completely eliminating three measured toxins - benzene, a known carcinogen, plus toluene and naphthalene. Temperatures of around 200° C. appear to be most efficient for vaporization. The potency of the cannabis in the study was on the order of 10% - 12%. Significant amounts of THC (around 5%-6%) begin to be released at 180° C., with slightly more (7% or 8%) at 200° C. Carbon monoxide and smoke tars were both qualitatively reduced by the vaporizer.

Medical Effects not related to Psychoactive Effects

Patients can obtain the medical benefits of cannabis, before any debilitating feelings of intoxication or 'high' take effect. Although users generally like to feel stoned, it is not necessary to experience full cannabis intoxication to benefit from the drug. By carefully monitoring the dosage, medical cannabis users can achieve a balance between intoxication and relief, in much the same way as controlled doses of morphine are administered to patients.

Chapter 18

MEDICAL CANNABIS

Truth can never be told so as to be understood, and not be believed. W. Blake, 1757-1827

Cannabis was highly valued in ancient medicine and its use can be traced back to the early classical physicians, Discorides and Galen; who reported that it relieved a wide variety of medical disorders. Today cannabis use is principally recreational, and the medical community remains cautious over its value as a medicine, primarily due to the prohibition argument. Divisions also exist within the medical cannabis lobby, with many protesting that people exploit the campaign with little interest in helping medical users. The medicinal use of cannabis is seen by many as a backdoor to legalisation and attracts individuals with purely commercial interests who see the moral high ground as a good way of promoting themselves or their business interests, at the expense of genuine medical activists like Colin Davies, imprisoned in the UK for openly supplying medicinal cannabis to patients.

Scientific data within the medical debate is also commonly misrepresented, although both sides are in agreement that cannabis is a powerful drug with differing effects. Dried cannabis plants vary in dosage, depending on the variety and growing conditions, therefore it is difficult to quantify dried and cured cannabis in the same way that regulators oversee other medications. The well-known psychological effects of cannabis use are a sense of well-being or euphoria and increased talkativeness and laughter, alternating with periods of introspective dreaminess, lethargy and sleepiness. Although many medical users consider these undesirable side effects, mood enhancement, anxiety reduction, and mild sedation can be useful for some patients. Cannabis has no potential for overdose; however, inexperienced or chronic cannabis users can experience acute, adverse mood reactions to large doses. Anxiety and paranoia is the most common; others include panic, agoraphobia, depression, dysphoria, depersonalisation, delusions, illusions, and hallucinations. The reactions don't last long, yet 17% of surveyed cannabis smokers reported experience of at least one of these symptoms. Cannabis use can also cause rapid heart beat *(tachycardia)* in humans, 20 to 100% above normal. The increase in heart rate is highest in the first 20 minutes after smoking then decreases rapidly, depending on dose. In contrast, chronic oral ingestion of cannabis reduces heart rate in humans. A change in heart rate and blood pressure present serious problems for some patients, but cannabis has no proven long-term health risks associated with its use and has no serious potential for dependency. However, withdrawal symptoms have been observed. In one study, subjects were given very high doses of oral THC: 180 to 210 mg per day for 10 to 20 days, (equivalent to smoking 9 to 10, 2% THC cigarettes per day). Once cannabis use stopped, the subjects were irritable and suffered mild insomnia, runny nose, sweating, and decreased appetite. The withdrawal symptoms lasted four days yet there was no associated craving for the drug, unlike cocaine amphetamines, opiates, alcohol and tobacco. Cannabis users should avoid *joints* that mix cannabis and tobacco due to the carcinogenic effect that tobacco has on the human body, in addition tobacco smoke contains many other harmful additives including sulphur and ammonia. The safest methods of ingestion for medicinal cannabis users are vaporisers or cooking with it.

Disorders that cannabis use can alleviate are;

AIDS

The body has no defence against *Acquired Immune Deficiency Syndrome* because the complex virus attacks the very cells that help the body to fight disease. Symptoms can include weight loss, fever, exhaustion and swollen glands. Patients suffer infections to their lungs, skin, nervous and digestive systems along with cancerous tumours and cannabis helps alleviate these and relieve pain. Some *HIV* carriers never go on to develop full-blown AIDS and this is helped by a healthy, stress free lifestyle coupled with a positive mental outlook. Sufferers report a feeling of well-being and contentment from cannabis use.

Aphrodisiac

Cannabis is a natural aphrodisiac and whilst it has no proven effect on male impotence it can greatly assist patients who are suffering from low *libido.*

Alzheimer's Disease

Sufferers experience a gradual mental degeneration late in life and cannabis has been shown to slow down the rate of deterioration in some patients. It is thought to reduce users risks of developing the disease.

Arthritis

There are more than 100 different types of arthritis that all involve some disorder of the joints. The two most common are *osteo* and *rheumatoid* arthritis and women are more susceptible than men. Patients suffer pain, swelling and deformation of their hips, knees, spines and hands, muscles are weakened, and tissues, tendons and ligaments become inflamed. Cannabis use eases the pain and discomfort of these attacks and slows deformation.

Asthma

Asthma attacks occur when inflammation or muscular spasms cause the bronchial passage of the lungs to contract, making breathing difficult. Other symptoms are coughing, wheezing, increased pulse rate and in some cases the patient will go blue in the face. Mostly the patient is panic stricken and pale. 85% of Asthma sufferers can alleviate their symptoms through smoking cannabis.

Cancerous Tumours

These are proliferations of swollen tissue. The use of cannabis can help in the control of many benign and cancerous tumours and alleviate the nausea associated with chemotherapy treatment

Cystic Fibrosis

This is caused by an inherited genetic disorder that starts when two *genes* fail to function. Symptoms are disruption of the exocrine glands that affects the pancreas, intestine, bronchial and sweat glands. Breathing and digestion are impaired by mucus. Cannabis is a local analgesic and will relieve symptoms.

Dementia

Moderate cannabis use is thought to delay the onset of dementia in elderly patients, but is not recommended for those with cardiovascular problems.

Depression

Cannabis has been successfully used to treat depression and is less habit forming than antidepressant drugs available on prescription. Cannabis has a euphoric effect on the nervous system.

Emphysema

This is a gradual deterioration of the lungs caused by heavy cigarette smoking and pollution. It occurs when the lung's tiny air sacs become distended and rupture. This makes the lungs less elastic and inefficient, as a result the heart has to work harder pumping blood through the system, leading to heart attacks and failure. Symptoms include breathlessness and blue lips. Research has shown that cannabis smoke inhaled into the lungs can relieve the symptoms associated with emphysema as it causes an expansion of the *bronchi* and *bronchioles* leading to higher oxygenation.

Epilepsy

The two most common are Grand Mal and Petit Mal. Grand Mal usually affects adults who can froth at the mouth and are in danger of swallowing their tongues. Petit Mal affects young children and teenagers. They can be so brief that the sufferer is unaware they have had a fit, as they only lose consciousness for a few seconds. In 60% of all epilepsy cases cannabis would have a positive effect on the sufferer. The extract of cannabis has been proven to be more effective than prescription drugs in reducing the frequency of fits.

Glaucoma

Cannabis is one of the most effective treatments for glaucoma, an eye disorder caused by an increase in intraocular pressure. This condition can lead to complete loss of sight. Cannabis can help 90% of glaucoma sufferers, as its effect on intraocular pressure is three times as high as prescription drugs, without any side effects.

Herpes

There is no cure for herpes and patients will continue to suffer attacks for life, however the severity diminishes with time. THC helps kill the herpes virus when it comes into contact with it. This is not a cure but sufferers report reduced recurrences of attacks when using cannabis. A topical application can reduce the healing time for herpes blisters.

High Blood Pressure

Blood pressure affects the rate at which the heart has to work. Abnormally high blood pressure is known as hypertension and usually affects middle-aged men. Cannabis extends the arteries and causes a reduction in pressure.

Insomnia

Sufferers have found that cannabis ingested an hour before sleep has a less stupefying effect than prescription drugs, gives the user a better quality of sleep and has no hangover, residual drowsiness.

Migraines

The first sign of an attack can be visual disturbance such as bright spots or jagged lines before the eyes followed by a severe one-sided headache. Migraines stem from a convulsive narrowing of the arteries. The consumption of cannabis eases attacks by reversing this effect.

Multiple Sclerosis

Symptoms can vary from lack of coordination through to slurred speech and incontinence. The muscular spasms and twitching that are associated with muscular sclerosis can be significantly reduced through cannabis use.

Muscular Cramping

Cannabis when smoked or used in a topical ointment is one of the best morphine free antispasmodic that is available.

Nausea

Cannabis can be used to treat nausea in patients undergoing chemotherapy treatments and acts as an appetizer for patients with eating disorders as well as those with pancreas and intestinal problems.

Pain

After nausea and vomiting, chronic pain is the condition cited most as a medical use for cannabis. Research in Southern California, USA has shown cannabinoids to be beneficial in the control of pain. Cannabinoids can be used alone or combined with opiates.

Post Traumatic Stress Disorder

Cannabis can be used in the treatment of traumatic stress sufferers who report benefits from using it to treat the psychological symptoms such as depression, anger and rage. Cannabis has a euphoric effect on the body and has no hangover or potential for dependency as with some prescription drugs.

Schizophrenia

In a recent study, schizophrenic patients were found to prefer cannabis to other drugs available; including alcohol and cocaine, which they were found to use less frequently than average. The reasons for this are unknown, but schizophrenics may be able to obtain some relief from moderate cannabis use. People with schizophrenia are more likely to suffer adverse psychiatric effects from chronic cannabis use.

Tourette's Syndrome

In extreme cases this psychiatric disorder causes uncontrollable spitting, shouting and swearing. It is very distressing for sufferers, who are otherwise perfectly normal. Researchers have discovered that cannabis use reduces the compulsion to behave in socially inappropriate ways.

Chapter 19

COMMERCIAL HEMP

Forgive them father for they know not what they do. Luke XXIII. 34

Cannabis sativa or hemp is grown as a bast or long fibre crop that is similar to flax. Humans have cultivated fibre hemp for thousands of years in a variety of different regions for its fibrous outer bark, its inner core (known as hurd) and its seeds. Archaeological evidence shows traces of hemp cultivation as early as 8,000 BC, with hemp textile production starting at the same point as the production of pottery. Hemp played a vital role in human development, providing clothing, fibre and animal feed. Where other fibres would have decayed rapidly in the saltwater spray, hemp was strong enough for sails, rope rigging and caulking, enabling man to travel across oceans. The Romans used hemp ropes and sails produced in Gaul (France). Although hemp was not grown in Ancient Rome, Lucilius documented its use in 120 BC, and Pliny the Elder outlined its preparation and different grades in the first century AD. Henry the VIII's promotion of the cultivation of hemp in England to support the navy and the maritime supremacy of Elizabethan times caused demand to grow.

Farmers who grow hemp regularly lose part of their harvest to people who think commercial hemp can be used in the same way as cannabis. One misguided gang I met whilst in a European prison had hired three cube vans and spent an entire night stealing a sizeable portion of one unfortunate farmer's hemp crop, only to discover once it had dried that they had a storeroom full of compost and stalks.

Hemp is sown in the spring and is an extremely fast-growing crop - reaching heights of almost 4 metres in about 110 days - and requires no herbicides or pesticides. Hemp is such a rapidly developing plant that it requires granular fertilizers or manure to maintain its vigour.

Hemp strips the ground of nutrients but with careful management and good soil preparation each season, crops can be grown continuously on the same land. The strong roots help to anchor the soil and control erosion. Fibre hemp is planted in dense rows to encourage tall, upright growth and this method of planting ensures that very little foliage is produced. As the plants mature, the leafy tops form a dense canopy that blocks out light and chokes weed growth, leaving the field in good condition for the following season. Fibre hemp is usually harvested before the onset of flowering to ensure optimum fibre quality. After harvest, the foliage is turned back into the soil; this process returns nutrients to the fields and that means less fertilizer is required the following season.

Fibre hemp differs from cannabis that has been bred for its psychoactive THC content. Cannabis varieties have up to 50 times the THC content of hemp varieties. Good cannabis plants contain around 15% THC, and some skunk varieties contain much higher levels. In contrast, fibre hemp varieties typically contains less than 0.3% THC. Throughout history, hemp has provided man with the strongest natural fibres available. Although traditionally used to make ropes and cloth, up until 1883 almost 90% of the world's paper was made from hemp fibre. Hemp paper lasts several times longer than wood pulp papers yet 95% of the world's paper is still made from trees as a direct result of the prohibition of cannabis cultivation. Hemp yields more than four times as much sustainable pulp per acre as timber. Each ton of paper made from hemp saves 12 mature trees and processing hemp uses fewer acids than processing wood pulp, thereby reducing pollution. Prohibition of cannabis cultivation has led to the destruction of thousands of acres of forests every year, purely to make wood pulp for paper. If we were to stop using trees for paper production, we would still be destroying our rainforests for timber to be used in the construction industry. The majority of our concrete buildings require formwork to provide moulds for the wet concrete, which are traditionally constructed from plywood. Hemp stalks can be chipped and processed into fibreboards that actually perform better than marine-ply and can be reused. In France, a hemp product called Isochanvre has been used as a replacement for concrete in construction and, although one seventh of the weight of concrete, it has greater shock resistance. Hemp pulp and fibre also offer a biodegradable alternative to plastic for many uses and can be polymerised without the use of petroleum. Advancements and innovation in hemp products and uses are restricted by prohibition. For example, hemp is perfect for the production of biomass fuel that is cleaner than fossil fuels, contains no sulphur, and can provide petroleum and methane that could meet all of our industrial and transportation needs. Cars could quite easily be adapted to run on cannabis fuels. Hemp oils can be used as a replacement for synthetic solvents. Prohibition prevents this and contributes to world pollution.

Hemp seeds were traditionally used to make a high protein seed cake for animal feed. They are more nutritious than Soya and far more digestible, causing less gas production in the gut. Hemp seeds could provide a complete source of vegetable protein for humans. The seeds contain about 30% oil by volume that can be extracted and used in cooking. Prohibition deprives us of a good supply of nutritious vegetable protein that contains high levels of edestin and albumin.

Fabrics made from hemp are stronger, more durable, have higher insulation properties, and are more absorbent and longer lasting than cotton. Hemp fibre holds its shape like polyester, but breathes in the same way as expensive man-made materials such as Gortex. It can be spun into a fine silk-like fibre or woven into coarse sacking such as burlap.

Hemp is one of the most versatile and durable materials we have, and, if used to its full potential, it could drastically reduce the effects of pollution and deforestation on our planet. Despite its potential, however, our elected governments largely prohibit hemp use because people enjoy the cannabis plant's intoxicating effects.

It is a strange world we make for ourselves.

"These are draconian laws, designed to relieve people like you of your money"

His Honour Judge Julian Hall

UK Forensic Science Service, Drugs Team.

Growers, when caught, will often claim that cultivation is for their own use or so-called "social supply" as opposed to being a commercial enterprise. Medicinal use is also used increasingly as an explanation for cannabis abuse. Such instances are generally on a scale of around 100 or more plants. Proof of the intent to supply cannabis to others in such cases depends on the number of plants, quality of cannabis produced and the sophistication of cultivation. In such instances, investigating officers may require a scientist to visit the site to assess the degree and sophistication of the cultivation and select plants and other items for examination and analysis. Although it is often all too apparent that a production site is commercial, it may be difficult to show an individual's involvement. Statements of evidence as well as description of the cannabis factory and relevant findings usually give some opinion of the potential yield of useable cannabis from the plants growing there and of their quality or THC content. Questions posed in court often relate to the estimated yield, e.g. whether it is a true estimate, whether it is an amount acceptable for personal use, taking into account the habit of the grower or whether such a yield is more likely to be supplied for commercial gain. Questions regarding the quality and value of the cannabis are also important. The cost of the equipment used and the degree of sophistication of the laboratory is significant, as the grower is often unemployed. Similarly, technical questions such as whether the plants have been grown from cuttings or seeds may also be important, especially if the plants have not yet flowered, 50 per cent of plants grown from seed may be male.

Quoted passage from academic work in public domain by C. Bone and S. J. Waldron, "Cannabis cultivation and abuse in the UK", Bulletin on Narcotics (UN publication)

Chapter 20

AND FINALLY

There are a lot of psychopaths in prison; unfortunately most are on the staff!
Craig Charles

In a truly free society there should be no laws to protect citizens from themselves. If an individual wants to grow and use cannabis plants then he or she should be free to do so: it is their choice. It seems incredible that by choosing to grow cannabis, individuals will be prosecuted by the state. In most of Europe, there is a tolerance of recreational cannabis use, and a person arrested for the first time with a small amount of personal cannabis will usually be cautioned and have the drug confiscated. Cultivators are generally prosecuted, which results in confiscation of the equipment and a fine or imprisonment (or both). If a person is shown to have benefited from dealing in cannabis the prosecution will attempt to seize their assets. Serious cultivators should keep nothing on paper and only keep small amounts of money in the bank.

If You Are Arrested

The usual procedure is that the police are made aware that an individual is cultivating or dealing in cannabis. The senior officer makes an evaluation as to the scale of the enquiry. The response will be calculated based on this evaluation. If it is suspected that the individual is growing a small amount for their own consumption, the police will decide to raid the premises where they believe cultivation is taking place.

If, after the evaluation by a senior officer, they decide that you are producing or dealing in cannabis on a larger scale, then the next stage will be to put you under observation to assess the scale of your operation and to build a picture of you and your associates. Whatever happens, the arrest will probably be the first you know about the operation against you. Raids often take place first thing in the morning, unless there are exceptional circumstances. You will be awakened by loud hammering on your front door, or the sound of the door being forcibly removed. If you want some good advice, buy a dog. My English bull terrier once held off an entire section of officers from the tactical firearms unit who tried to storm my back garden. All you could see was a row of black baseball caps peeking over the fence.

But be warned, the majority of these officers are failed Rambos who have found a way to live out their fantasies, and they are dangerous. They will use CS gas against your dogs, which is very distressing. The gas attacks moist areas of the body and dogs will convulse and howl in agony. They gassed my friend's Staffordshire bulls through the letterbox, before smashing down his door to search for cannabis. Once they have gained access to your property they will arrest you. By this stage they are excited, just stay calm. The arresting officer will explain that you are under arrest and say why. Do not say anything at this stage. A search of your premises will then take place at which you may or may not be present. Just say nothing. You will then be taken to a police station where you will be processed and searched. Ask to speak to a lawyer, and do not say anything else. After processing you will be put in a cell with a thin, plastic-covered mattress. Lie on the mattress and try to sleep. Even though this is the last thing on your mind, it gives you an opportunity to collect your thoughts. Police procedure is to check on the prisoner in custody and report this to the investigating officers. They hate it when you are relaxed and asleep. Do not say or do anything until you have spoken to your lawyer. It is always better to say nothing and argue that you were confused or fearful in the police station. You may want to make a statement to the police in which case you must never tell the truth or give information on anyone. Play down any cultivation you have been involved in and any profits that you have made. The police are interested in figures and will provide their own experts to say that you have benefited from ridiculous amounts. Don't worry about this either, the first thing any competent barrister or lawyer will do is commission an independent forensic expert to examine the evidence in your case. The police will try to trick you into admitting to supplying cannabis to others. If you have been arrested with a small amount, maintain that it was for your own personal use and you never intended to pass it on to another person, even as a gift.

After being interviewed by the investigating officers, you will either be released on police bail or charged with the offences. Being charged with an offence does not preclude you from police bail, but if the offence is deemed serious enough you will be remanded into custody. A remand into custody means that you will appear before a local magistrate the next day. They sanction the decision the police have already made. You are then taken to a local prison where you will enter the reception area, be processed, assigned a wing, and once again locked in a cell. Imprisonment is not to be feared. It allows you time to think and prepare your defence, but please, never discuss your case with anyone except your legal advisors or co-accused, and even then be careful. The authorities regularly use other inmates as informants and there have been many cases where inmates have given evidence against fellow prisoners in exchange for lighter sentences.
To the police, information is a valuable commodity and they are prepared to trade for it. All of the defendants in my case were approached and offered deals; the only one who claimed not to have been asked had already taken the deal. I told them nothing; it's not what I'm about. You choose certain paths in life and must take responsibility for your choices. Unfortunately, there are weak individuals who fail to grasp this concept. Even the police despise them and that is saying something when you consider how corrupt, racist, and dishonest some officers are. British detectives took £5,000 in cash from my partner's house on our last arrest. They thought he wouldn't declare it but it was legal money from his shop. When his lawyer demanded its return they denied ever seizing it and threatened his wife with prosecution. The money is still missing.

While I was in prison, four London drug squad detectives wearing hoods were arrested in the early hours of the morning breaking into a lockup garage to steal a consignment of cannabis that had been stored there by dealers. They hadn't known that the area was under surveillance by another police squad.

Even if you have been caught in possession of large amounts of cannabis, do not give up. Think your case through. Are there likely to have been informants in the case? If so, do you have an idea as to who they might be? Police procedure is to protect informants at all costs, they must do this or no other informants will come forward, and this is to the defendant's advantage. A defence of duress exists in most countries. If the defendant can convince a jury that at the time the offence was committed the accused was in fear of his or her life and only acting because they were threatened by another person or persons, then the accused is not guilty of that offence. It can suit the defence to say that the offence was only committed because the informant threatened the defendant who, as a result of this threat, was in fear for their life. This defence allows your lawyer or barrister to call and cross-examine the informant in open court. The prosecution cannot allow this because they know that if your legal team asks the witness if he or she is a police informant, they must answer truthfully or perjure themselves. Prosecution counsel will drop a case rather than disclose the identity of any informants. If you have no idea who the informants are, and have no defence, then a guilty plea can earn you a certain discount off your sentence for saving the court time and money. Ensure that your legal team plays down the sums of money involved and have their own forensic scientists back this up. This is where any statement you may have made can be useful, especially if the police have only found equipment and not plants, as you can claim what you like. The judge in my case remarked that if the court were to believe what I was saying, it would appear I had lost £10,000 since starting cultivating. At one point he lost all composure and shouted 'Liar' at my co-accused. If you suffer from any of the illnesses that cannabis can alleviate be sure to mention them in court and if you don't have any, develop one.

When you enter a plea of "not guilty" it means you then have to face a trial before a jury. You will be represented by a lawyer or barrister who will argue your case before the court and cross-examine witnesses on your behalf. It is entirely possible for defendants to represent themselves in court but doing so is not advised unless you are competent with legal procedures.

A defendant is under no obligation to give evidence during the trial itself and I know of cases where barristers have advised their clients not to do so. This is invariably a mistake, as juries tend to assume that if you will not answer the prosecution's questions you have something to hide. It is important to appear in the dock and to tell your side of the story. The prosecutor will use a variety of techniques to show you to be a liar before turning to the jury and claiming that they should believe nothing you have said.

Important Hints for When You're Being Cross Examined

Do not allow the prosecutor to rush you through questions to confuse you. Keep asking them to repeat the question to allow you time to think. Say, "I am sorry I did not hear / understand you, can you repeat the question please?" This frustrates their efforts. Always pause and think before answering.

Do not allow the prosecutor to draw you into any arguments and don't lose your temper. Consistently deny all the allegations with a firm but polite: "No, that simply is not true." It is very difficult for a prosecutor to unsettle you if you adopt this approach.

If you cannot remember a specific fact or detail then say so, and only give facts and details that you are sure of. Believe any facts you are giving them.

If a prosecutor continues to go over points you have answered, turn to the judge and say, "Your honour I've answered this question several times." The judge won't like it but will direct the prosecutor to move on. Don't spend your time planning answers to specific questions that may or may not be asked. You know the direction in which your defence is to go, so always answer the prosecution's points with this in mind. Stay focused and stay strong.

L.homme est ne'libre et partout il est dans les fers
Man is born free, and everywhere he is in chains
Jean-Jacques Rousseau , 1712-1778.

Online Privacy (Encryption / Firewalls)

"Privacy is a fundamental human right, recognized as such by the United Nations. We risk being struck a crippling, irreparable blow if we allow ourselves to become subjected to constant, unrelenting surveillance and observation by the police or any other agents of the state".
George Radwanski

Why do I need encryption?

The internet is inherently unsafe. Once you computer is online your connection is a two way highway. Others can read your messages and access all pictures and files on your hard drive / generally called Drive (C).

Can someone get onto my computer and look around?

Yes! Police and security services / computer hackers / private detectives / employers / computer repairmen may have already done so. Protect your computer itself with a firewall programme such as **ZONE ALARM**. Use encryption to protect files on your hard disc and when e-mailing anything you wouldn't want others to read.

What is encryption?

It is a type of programme you install on your computer that codes images or text files so that only those with a secure password can view them. You can download a variety of encryption programmes free from this books website.

Online Privacy (Proxy Server)

Why do I need a Proxy server?

Every computer that connects to the internet has what is called an **IP Address**. This address can be used to identify you. Every time you visit a website you leave a digital footprint that can be followed. You can hide your IP address and surf invisibly by using a **Proxy Server** (basically you surf via the proxy whose own IP is displayed instead of yours). If you are using Internet Explorer it is easy to set up a proxy.
(1) Find a list of Proxy Servers from the internet. These are freely available at **http://www.stayinvisible.com.**
(2) Whilst connected to the internet open Internet Explorer and click on **Tools** / **Internet options.**
(3) Click on **Connections** / highlight your connection device *(Freeserve, aol etc)*
(4) Click **Settings**. Another box will pop up, click **Use a proxy server** and enter the IP address of your chosen proxy, and a port.
(5) Cut and paste the same IP and port into your **Settings** box, click **OK.**
(6) Do an **Environment Check** (basically check the proxy is working as they die after a few days and need replacing). If nothing loads the proxy is dead so find another one and repeat the process.

ONLINE

Education is an admirable thing. Oscar Wilde, 1854-1900.

Included with this book is a password that allows you access to the books free webpages. This can be found at:

http://www.cyberskunk.net

You can login and download free information, software, images, articles and games. Enter the details below when prompted:

Your Username is: **cyberskunk**
Your password is: **amsterdam**

Useful URLs

Seeds
www.seedsdirect.to
www.high-land.co.uk
www.amazing-nature.com
www.sensiseeds.com

Hydroponics / Grow equipment
www.21stcenturygarden.co.uk
www.theorganicgrowshop.co.uk
www.evergreenhydroponics.co.uk
www.thegardensuperstore.co.uk

Electronics / Vents / Lowbays
www.maplin.co.uk
www.screwfix.com
www.fastlight.co.uk

Generators
www.hondadirect.co.uk
www.kw1.com

Campaigners
www.ccguide.org.uk
www.norml.org
www.maps.org

Security
www.stayinvisible.com
www.anonymizer.com

Grow information
www.uk420.com
www.hempcity.net
www.overgrow.com
www.sweetleaf.co.uk
www.highlife.nl

Headshops
www.everyonedoesit.com
www.avalonheadshop.co.uk
www.tangygifts.co.uk

Books / Magazines
www.freedombooks.co.uk
www.amazon.co.uk

Aquarium pumps / carbon
www.aquatics-warehouse.co.uk
www.aquarium-supplies.co.uk

Appendix 2

GLOSSARY

Imagination is more important than knowledge, Albert Einstein 1879–1955

Aeroponics - growing plants by misting roots suspended in a light-proof chamber.
Acetone - solvent chemical used in the extraction of oil from cannabis.
Ballast - used to control *HID* lights. Can be housed in the light unit itself as with *Poot* horticultural lamps, or as a separate remote unit.
Bhang - a drink made from cannabis.
Bonsai - pruned and shaped, small plant.
Botrytis - a fungal infection that attacks plants. Is easily identified by a grey fluffy growth on the affected part. Particularly damaging during flowering and will ruin a crop (see *troubleshooting Pests and fungi*).
Calyx - seed pod containing the female ovule and two emerging pistils.
Capillary action - refers to the tendency of liquid to be drawn up or through a plant or a material.
CF - the ability of a liquid to conduct a current. Used to measure the amount of dissolved nutrients in a solution.
Chillum - a small pipe used to smoke cannabis.
Chlorophyll - the green colouring matter of plants.
Chlorosis - the name given to the condition whereby a plant appears pale and has thin leaves and stems. Caused by insufficient light levels.
Colchicine - a chemical used to induce polyploidy in cannabis.
Cytokinins - hormones found in sea plants.
Defoliation - process in which leaves are stripped from a healthy growing plant to induce shock and polyploidy that can increase yields.
Dioecious - the term used to describe species that have separate male and female plants.
Dronabidol - the brand name given to synthesized THC.
Ethylene - A naturally occurring gas given off by many ripening vegetables and fruit.
Feminised - the process in which seeds are treated to produce more females than males.
Gene - part of a chromosome that influences the structure of your plants.
Ghee - indian name for clarified butter.
Hashish - pressed extract of cannabis.
Hermaphrodites - plants that develop both male and female flowers.
Hormone - chemical substance that controls the growth and development of cannabis plants.
HPS - high pressure sodium light
Humidity - the measurement of water held in the atmosphere.
Humus - decayed living matter in the soil.
Hybrid - offspring from two plants of different breeds.
Hygrometer - instrument used to measure the relative humidity of an area.
Hypocotyl - the name given to the stem that emerges from the seed case and pushes up towards the light.
Internode - The point on the plant where side shoots develop.
Lumen - measurement of light output
Manicuring - trimming the leaves from around the dried cannabis.
Marijuana - word used to describe cannabis (word has racist origins in the US).
Marinol - see Dronabidol.
MH - metal Halide lights used in indoor cultivation.
Moraceae - the family to which the cannabis plant belongs. Hemp is classified as cannabis sativa.
NPK - used to classify fertilizer by its nutrient content.
Oestrogen - a chemical used in the production of birth control pills.
Papaver somniferum - latin name for the opium poppy.
pH - a measurement of acidity or alkalinity.
Phytochrome - hormone responsible for regulating the growing and flowering stages of the cannabis plant.
Pistils – thin white hairs that emerge from the female pods on the female cannabis plants when they flower.
Polyploid - genetic mutations in plant species.
Resin - see Hashish.
Sinsimella - word meaning ‘seedless’ used to refer to a crop of female cannabis.

THC4MS

URGENT APPEAL

TO THE GROWING COMMUNITY

THC4MS supplies medicinal cannabis chocolate to bonefide MS sufferers in emergency situations only i.e.:- As a first point of contact or their normal supply is exhausted, although many of our patients are supplied on a regular basis as they are unable to produce their own medi-canna-chocolate.

THC4MS relies upon donations of raw herbal cannabis from the UK underground growing community to produce our product, we never have and hopefully never will have to buy in supplies of herbal cannabis.

THC4MS now has over 600 regular recipients of our product and the numbers are rising daily, if we are to continue being able to supply all of these people on a regular basis we need your help now.

PLEASE if you are producing your own quality herbal cannabis at home we NEED your help to continue operating our FREE service. Please consider donating a small percentage of your crop to be redistributed to the medicinal cannabis community.

For more information about our service, please visit our website WWW.THC4MS.ORG.UK

If you would like to make a donation please contact us via e-mail help@thc4ms.org.uk in the first instance.

ALL DONATIONS GO DIRECTLY TO MEDICINAL USERS
NO WAGES OR FAVOURS ARE EVER PAID

WE LOOK FORWARD TO HEARING FROM YOU